WISDOM

THE JESUS CLASSICS

AT A GLANCE

Serendipity House / P.O. Box 1012 / Littleton, CO 80160
TOLL FREE 1-800-525-9563 / www.serendipityhouse.com
© 1989, 1999 Serendipity House. All rights reserved.
SECOND EDITION
00 01 02 / **201 series • CHG** / 4 3 2

PROJECT ENGINEER:
Lyman Coleman

WRITING TEAM:
Richard Peace, Lyman Coleman, Matthew Lockhart, Andrew Sloan, Cathy Tardif

PRODUCTION TEAM:
Christopher Werner, Sharon Penington, Erika Tiepel

COVER PHOTO:
© 1998 Karen Evenson, Stock Imagery, Inc.

CORE VALUES

Community:	The purpose of this curriculum is to build community within the body of believers around Jesus Christ.
Group Process:	To build community, the curriculum must be designed to take a group through a step-by-step process of sharing your story with one another.
Interactive Bible Study:	To share your "story," the approach to Scripture in the curriculum needs to be open-ended and right brain—to "level the playing field" and encourage everyone to share.
Developmental Stages:	To provide a healthy program in the life cycle of a group, the curriculum needs to offer courses on three levels of commitment: (1) Beginner Stage—low-level entry, high structure, to level the playing field; (2) Growth Stage—deeper Bible study, flexible structure, to encourage group accountability; (3) Discipleship Stage—in-depth Bible study, open structure, to move the group into high gear.
Target Audiences:	To build community throughout the culture of the church, the curriculum needs to be flexible, adaptable and transferable into the structure of the average church.

ACKNOWLEDGMENTS

To Zondervan Bible Publishers
for permission to use
the NIV text,
The Holy Bible, New International Bible Society.
© 1973, 1978, 1984 by International Bible Society.
Used by permission of Zondervan Bible Publishers.

Questions & Answers

STAGE

1. What stage in the life cycle of a small group is this course designed for?

Turn to the first page of the center section of this book. There you will see that this 201 course is designed for the second stage of a small group. In the Serendipity "Game Plan" for the multiplication of small groups, your group is in the Growth Stage.

GOALS

2. What are the goals of a 201 study course?

As shown on the second page of the center section (page M2), the focus in this second stage is equally balanced between Bible Study, Group Building, and Mission / Multiplication.

BIBLE STUDY

3. What is the approach to Bible Study in this course?

Take a look at page M3 of the center section. The objective in a 201 course is to discover what a book of the Bible, or a series of related Scripture passages, has to say to our lives today. We will study each passage seriously, but with a strong emphasis on practical application to daily living.

THREE-STAGE LIFE CYCLE OF A GROUP

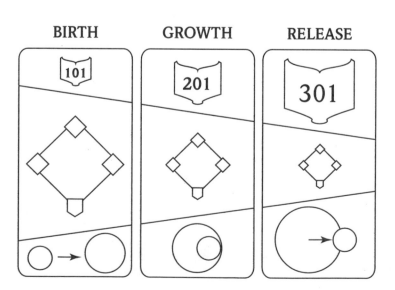

GROUP BUILDING

4. *What is the meaning of the baseball diamond on pages M2 and M3 in relation to Group Building?*

Every Serendipity course includes group building. First base is where we share our own stories; second base means affirming one another's stories; third base is sharing our personal needs; and home plate is deeply caring for each others' needs. In this 201 course we will continue "checking in" with each other and holding each other accountable to live the Christian life.

MISSION / MULTIPLICATION

5. *What is the mission of a 201 group?*

The mission of this 201 Covenant group is to discover the future leaders for starting a new group. (See graph on the previous page.) During this course, you will be challenged to identify three people and let this team use the Bible Study time to practice their skills. The center section will give you more details.

THE EMPTY CHAIR

6. *How do we fill "the empty chair"?*

First, pull up an empty chair during the group's prayer time and ask God to bring a new person to the group to fill it. Second, have everyone make a prospect list of people they could invite and keep this list on their refrigerator until they have contacted all those on their list.

AGENDA

7. *What is the agenda for our group meetings?*

A three-part agenda is found at the beginning of each session. Following the agenda and the recommended amount of time will keep your group on track and will keep the three goals of Bible Study, Group Building, and Mission / Multiplication in balance.

THE FEARLESS FOURSOME

If you have more than seven people at a meeting, Serendipity recommends you divide into groups of 4 for the Bible Study. Count off around the group: "one, two, one, two, etc."—and have the "ones" move quickly to another room for the Bible Study. Ask one person to be the leader and follow the directions for the Bible Study time. After 30 minutes, the Group Leader will call "Time" and ask all groups to come together for the Caring Time.

8. *How do we decide what ice-breakers to use to begin the meetings?*

Page M7 of the center section contains an index of ice-breakers in four categories: (1) those for getting acquainted in the first session or when a new person comes to a meeting; (2) those for the middle sessions to help you report in to your group; (3) those for the latter sessions to affirm each other and assign roles in preparation for starting a new group in the future; and (4) those for evaluating and reflecting in the final session.

9. *What is a group covenant?*

A group covenant is a "contract" that spells out your expectations and the ground rules for your group. It's very important that your group discuss these issues—preferably as part of the first session (see also page M32 in the center section).

10. *What are the ground rules for the group?* (Check those you agree upon.)

❐ PRIORITY: While you are in the course, you give the group meetings priority.

❐ PARTICIPATION: Everyone participates and no one dominates.

❐ RESPECT: Everyone is given the right to their own opinion and all questions are encouraged and respected.

❐ CONFIDENTIALITY: Anything that is said in the meeting is never repeated outside the meeting.

❐ EMPTY CHAIR: The group stays open to new people at every meeting.

❐ SUPPORT: Permission is given to call upon each other in time of need—even in the middle of the night.

❐ ADVICE GIVING: Unsolicited advice is not allowed.

❐ MISSION: We agree to do everything in our power to start a new group as our mission (see center section).

Introduction to Jesus' Parables

"He taught them many things by parables …" (Mark 4:2).

Jesus was a master storyteller. Whether he was addressing a large crowd on a hillside, sharing a private meal with his disciples, or answering one of the Pharisees' trick questions, Jesus would often use stories to make his point.

Jesus used other methods of teaching, of course. He gave lectures and sermons, he posed thought-provoking questions, and he debated and dialogued. But there was something unique about the stories he told. Though simple in form, these stories carried a deeper message that slowly penetrated the minds of his listeners until the truth of it exploded within them. Some people were enlightened and compelled to glorify God. Others were enraged when they realized what Jesus was really saying about them and about himself.

These stories—or *parables*—have a lasting quality about them. They not only challenged the original hearers to reconsider seriously their relationship to God, they also cause us to do the same. In this book, we will be studying 13 of Jesus' best-known parables. But before we begin, we need to consider a few details about parables in general— their meaning, purpose and interpretation.

What Is a Parable?

The English word "parable" comes from the Greek word *parabole,* which literally means "to place alongside." So, a parable compares one thing to another. In the Gospels, they are specifically used to compare some aspect of common, everyday life with some reality about the kingdom of God. However, parables are not simply illustrations (such as those found in modern speech or sermons). An illustration may help an audience understand or apply a point the speaker is making, but it is not in itself essential to what the speaker is trying to say; the main weight of the communication is carried by concepts and ideas. In contrast, *a parable is the message.* It is not used to illustrate the point; it *is* the point. In graphic, picturesque language the parable communicates insight about God, his kingdom, and the response expected of those who hear.

There is no single, uniform type of parable. In the Greek version of the Old Testament, the word parable is applied to proverbs (1 Sam. 10:12;

Prov. 1:1,6), riddles (Judg. 14:10–18), taunt songs (Mic. 2:4; Hab. 2:6–20) and allegories (Isa. 5:1–7; Ezek. 17:3–24).[1] The same broad use of the word is found in the New Testament, where parables range from short one-liners (i.e., "It is not the healthy who need a doctor, but the sick" —Mark 2:17) to extended narratives like the story of the Good Samaritan (Luke 10:25–37). Parables are not unique to Jesus. Parables such as those Jesus told can be found in the Old Testament, and in the literature of Jewish rabbis (prior to Jesus) who used parables as a means of teaching. While the breadth of the nature and purpose of parables makes definition difficult, there are two helpful definitions:

- A metaphor or simile drawn from life or nature which captures our interest (by being so vivid and strange) and leaves us just enough confused (and teased) to think deeply about what it exactly means for our lives.[2]

- A dramatic form of theological language that compels us to make a response, because it reveals the nature of the kingdom of God (or shows how a child of the kingdom should act).[3]

The Purpose of the Parables

Both definitions emphasize how the parables of Jesus call for response. Parables are not simply stories (like Aesop's fables) that reinforce the kind of moral values that contribute to a good life. Nor are they Zen riddles meant to unhinge our minds to prepare us to transcend levels of consciousness. Instead, as the second definition shows, their intent is to reveal something of the kingdom of God and to call the hearer to respond to Jesus and his mission. They describe what life in that kingdom is like. They portray something of the nature of the King. They call the listeners to decide how they will live in light of the presence of the King in their midst. As has been often observed, no one would have bothered to crucify an itinerant Jewish peasant who went around telling stories that encouraged proper moral behavior! No—the parables are stories of a new kingdom that stands against the old ways.

While it is popularly thought that Jesus used parables to simplify hard truths, the reality is that

the parables themselves were difficult to understand! As noted in the first definition, one mark of many of Jesus' parables is that they have a twist that would have been totally unexpected to his hearers, and disturbed their assumptions about the way things are. A Samaritan, despised by the orthodox Jews as unworthy of God, ends up as the hero in a story that includes a Jewish priest and a Levite. Despotic, fabulously wealthy kings, normally concerned only with their own power and wealth, mercifully cancel enormous debts owed to them by mere servants who have wasted the king's resources. People throw a party over the recovery of one stupid lamb that got lost from a herd. As Jesus speaks to the Middle Eastern listener of his day, he knows that none of these actions is normal. It is precisely these strange twists that make the parables like thought-bombs which are tossed into the lives of those who hear them. Some parables may have a short fuse and others may have a long one, but sooner or later the parable explodes, rocking the hearer with new awareness about the implications of Jesus and his kingdom. In these parables "the ordinary has gone askew and thereby shocks us into realizing that the parables lead into another way of thinking about life."[4]

Craig Blomberg provides a helpful summary of the overall purposes of the parables:

1. Jesus has three main topics of interest: the graciousness of God, the demands of discipleship, and the dangers of disobedience.

2. The central theme uniting all of the lessons of the parables is the kingdom of God. It is both present and future. … It involves both personal transformation and social reform. It is … the dynamic power of God's personal revelation of himself in creating a human community of those who serve Jesus in every area of their lives.

3. The teachings of the parables raise the question of Jesus' identity. Who is this one who, by his teaching, can claim to forgive sins, pronounce God's blessing on social outcasts, and declare that final judgment will be based on the responses people make to him?

4. Jesus' parables include implicit claims to deity. Jesus associates himself with authority figures in his parables (which obviously stand for the God of the Hebrew Scriptures). His audiences must decide whether to accept these claims and worship him, or to reject them as misguided or even blasphemous. But Jesus' parables leave no neutral ground for casual interest or idle curiosity. They sharply divided their original audiences into disciples and opponents. They must continue to function in the same way today.[5]

Interpreting the Parables

For much of the history of the church, the parables were seen as elaborate allegories. In an allegory, the details of a story have a deeper meaning that the reader must discern. While a few of the parables in the Gospels are interpreted allegorically by Jesus himself (i.e., Matt. 13:24–30,36–43), this approach to the parables led some interpreters to assign meanings to details that had no relation to anything that Jesus' original hearers would have understood. The danger in treating parables as allegories is that the parables can then be manipulated to support whatever theological interests are important to the reader, rather than allowing them to convey the original intention of Jesus.

The allegorical approach was finally challenged by leaders of the Reformation period. Calvin, Luther and others sought to understand parables within the context of Jesus' ministry. But even they often failed to understand much of what Jesus was saying. It wasn't until the nineteenth century that scholars began to study these teachings in light of the historical, cultural and theological realities of Jesus' time. Since then, in reaction to the excessive, fanciful allegorizing of the parables that dominated earlier periods of the church, the prevailing position has been that parables have *only one main point*, and that this point is somehow related to the kingdom of God. While this was a needed corrective, today there are scholars who argue that this perspective is too limited. These scholars have opened the way to looking for *multiple meanings* in the parables, not in the sense that they become imaginative allegories, but in the

sense that the various characters and situations in the parables are meant to embrace various theological themes that work together to evoke a response from the hearer.

Kenneth Bailey suggests several important principles to keep in mind in seeking to understand, interpret and apply a parable:

1. Determine the audience. Is Jesus talking to the scribes and Pharisees, to the crowds, or to his disciples? The meaning of the parable is related to the audience who heard it. The Parable of the Prodigal Son (Luke 15:11–32) takes on new meaning when it is realized that Jesus told it to a group of Pharisees who were appalled by his association with people they considered to be sinners. Knowing this, the fact that we are not told how the older brother in the story finally responds takes on a new significance. What on one level is the story of God's grace to sinners is, on another level, an open-ended challenge for these Pharisees (who are like the older brother) to repent.

2. Examine carefully the setting/interpretation provided by the author or his source. Most of the parables are found in the context of a particular setting which informs the meaning of the parable. For example, the parable about the generous moneylender (Luke 7:41–42) takes on special meaning when we see that it is found in the context of Jesus' encounter with a sinful woman and a self-righteous Pharisee. The context makes it clear that this simple story is a strong rebuke of the lack of love for God on the part of the Pharisee. It also forces the reader to ask questions regarding the authority and identity of Jesus, since he clearly places himself in the role of the one who forgives enormous debts owed to him.

3. Try to discern the cultural presuppositions of the story, keeping in mind that the people in them are Palestinian peasants. The point here is not only to identify Middle Eastern customs (such as what people wore or how they traveled), but also to become familiar with their values, their ways of relating to one another, and their sense of propriety. While in our culture we do not see anything particularly strange with older men running (they are either exercising or are about to miss their plane!),

older men in the Middle East always walked slowly as a sign of their dignity. This sheds new light on the detail in the Parable of the Prodigal Son which tells how the father *ran* to greet his son.

4. Try to discern what symbols the original audience would have instinctively identified in the parable. This process requires us to get into someone else's world. To speak of Santa Claus in the United States is to evoke a whole range of images and feelings that are culturally associated with Santa Claus. However, a man from China would not react the same way to such a comment, since Santa plays no part in Chinese culture. We do not immediately grasp the meanings of the symbols in the same way as the original listeners would have, because we do not share their culture. We have to work at it.

5. Determine what response the original audience is pressed to make in the original telling of the parable. As we see the effect the parable was intended to have upon its audience, we can consider what parallel effects it is to have upon us. St. Augustine's interpretation of the Parable of the Good Samaritan laid stress on the importance of getting people into the church in order to be saved. However, since the scribe who asked the question that prompted the parable (Luke 10:25–29) would have understood Jesus' story as a call for him to start acting as a neighbor to anyone in need, it is clear that Augustine's application is invalid. As important as the church is, involvement in it simply is not the topic of this parable.

6. Discern what the parable says about the cluster of theological themes that it affirms and/or presupposes. The parables reflect truths about God and how God expects his followers to live. Once we have identified the major symbols the original listeners would have understood and have discerned the response that the parable calls forth on the part of its listeners, we can discern the central truths about God and discipleship which are encapsulated within the parable. For example, Bailey suggests that the parable about the obedient servant in Luke 17:7–10 is built upon the assumptions that the believer is expected to obey God as his servant, that salvation is a gift not a

reward, that believers have no claim upon God, and that God is served as one obeys Jesus.

Some of these suggestions may make us feel that there is no way we can understand the parables. After all, most of us have no idea what cultural assumptions or values a Middle Eastern peasant at the time of Jesus might have had! Fortunately, this gap can be filled in through three main ways.

First, we can engage in thoughtful, careful reading of the text to see what it says and what it stresses. Discovering the context of a parable and the responses it generated among people is not difficult, since most of the parables occur in the middle of a bigger story. We can read around the parable to see how it fits into the bigger picture of what is happening. The more we read the Bible, the more familiar we will become with the way people thought and felt at the time. This will help us keep the parables in their historical context and protect us from reading our own thoughts and ideas into them.

Secondly, we can avail ourselves of the many excellent tools available to help us understand the background of the Bible and its ancient Middle Eastern culture. Bible dictionaries, commentaries, studies of the culture of biblical times (such as the *Life and Times of Jesus* by Alfred Eidersheim), and books on the parables are invaluable aids in this process. The notes that accompany each study are drawn from such resources and the Acknowledgments on page 63 provide a good reading list for more comprehensive study.

Thirdly, we can benefit from learning about Middle Eastern people and cultures of today. Kenneth Bailey points out that many of the peasant customs and attitudes in the Middle East today have remained relatively unchanged for centuries. The insights about relationships and values that we can learn from Middle Eastern people today can shed valuable light on the meaning of the parables.[6]

Conclusion

The parables remain a rich source of spiritual insight for us. While most North Americans are more used to hearing their theology expressed in *creeds and concepts* (such as "I believe in God the Father Almighty, maker of heaven and earth …" or "The chief purpose of man is to glorify God and enjoy him forever"), the parables present us with *pictures* of God and his kingdom. Like any good art, the parables communicate beyond their original audience. While rooted in the life and times of Jesus, the realities about God and discipleship that the parables present transcend that culture, and speak to us as well in images that are more powerful than words. We may well forget the formal definition of God (found in the catechisms that some of us were forced to memorize in church school), but we are not likely to forget the parable which tells us that God is like a shepherd who goes to great lengths to find his lost sheep. Those long sermons about what it really means to be a Christian may fade from our memory, but we will remember that the people of the kingdom are like the man who found a treasure buried in a field and in his joy sold all that he had in order to buy the field and gain the treasure. Theological discussions about the end times may leave us suspecting that everyone is really using Bible texts to suit their own perspectives, but we can find a clear word of hope in the assurance that the kingdom of God is like a little bit of yeast in a batch of dough which ends up influencing every part of that dough.

The parables are word pictures Jesus painted in order to teach us theology in a way that would stick with us. Once the parable is heard, it is etched in the mind, where the Spirit of God can, over time, reveal its deeper implications to us as we are prepared to hear them.

"He who has ears to hear, let him hear" (Mark 4:9).

[1]Kenneth Bailey, *The Gospel in Parable*, Fortress Press, 1988, p. 5.
[2]Adapted from C.H. Dodd, quoted in *The Gospel in Parable*, John Donahue, Fortress, 1988, p. 5.
[3]Adapted from Bailey, *Poet and Peasant: Through Peasant Eyes*, Eerdmans, 1983.
[4]op. cit., Donahue.
[5]Craig Blomberg, *Interpreting the Parables*, InterVarsity Press, pp. 326–327.
[6]Adapted from Bailey, pp. xxii–xxiii in *Poet and Peasant: Through Peasant Eyes.*

1 Pharisee's Prayer—Luke 18:9–14

THREE-PART AGENDA

ICE-BREAKER
15 Minutes

BIBLE STUDY
30 Minutes

CARING TIME
15–45 Minutes

> *LEADER: Be sure to read pages 3–5 in the front of this book, and go over the ground rules on page 5 with the group in this first session. See page M7 in the center section for a good ice-breaker. Have your group look at pages M1–M5 in the center section and fill out the team roster on page M5.*

TO BEGIN THE BIBLE STUDY TIME
(Choose 1 or 2)

1. Growing up, who said prayers with you at bedtime? What were your prayers like?

2. When do you usually pray: Before bed? At church? Behind the wheel? Before meals? Early in the morning? In times of crisis? Other?

3. How comfortable are you praying out loud in front of people?

READ SCRIPTURE & DISCUSS
(If you don't have time for all the questions in this section, conclude the Bible Study [30 min.] by answering question #7.)

1. Who is someone you look to as a model of how to pray and why?

2. In this parable, the Pharisee "prayed about himself" (v. 11). When you pray, what do you usually pray about?

3. How do you feel about the Pharisee in this parable? How do you feel about the tax collector? How would people in Jesus' day view the two characters in this parable (see notes on v. 10)?

The Parable of the Pharisee and the Tax Collector

⁹To some who were confident of their own righteousness and looked down on everybody else, Jesus told this parable: ¹⁰"Two men went up to the temple to pray, one a Pharisee and the other a tax collector. ¹¹The Pharisee stood up and prayed about[a] himself: 'God, I thank you that I am not like other men—robbers, evildoers, adulterers—or even like this tax collector. ¹²I fast twice a week and give a tenth of all I get.'

¹³"But the tax collector stood at a distance. He would not even look up to heaven, but beat his breast and said, 'God, have mercy on me, a sinner.'

¹⁴"I tell you that this man, rather than the other, went home justified before God. For everyone who exalts himself will be humbled, and he who humbles himself will be exalted."

[a] 11 Or to

4. Why did the tax collector go home "justified before God" (v. 14) rather than the Pharisee?

5. When have you been like the tax collector crying out, "God have mercy on me, a sinner" (v. 13)?

6. What point was Jesus making with this parable?

7. What brought you to this study and what are you hoping to get out of it?

CARING TIME

1. Have your group agree on its group covenant and ground rules (see page 5 in the front of this book)?

2. Work on filling out your team roster (see page M5 in the center section). Like any winning team, every position needs to be covered.

3. Who is someone you would like to invite to this group for next week?

P.S. At the close, pass around your books and have everyone sign the Group Directory inside the front cover.

Share prayer requests and close in prayer. Be sure to pray for "the empty chair" (p. 4).

Notes—Luke 18:9–14

Summary. This parable relates to the previous parable in Luke 18:1–8 in that it talks about prayer, but it really belongs more with the two scenes that follow it (Jesus with the little children in verses 15–17, and Jesus and the rich young ruler in verses 18–30). Both the parable and the scenes revolve around the fact that God's kingdom is given to a far different group of people (little children and the poor) than the ones traditionally thought to have earned it. The parable (vv. 9–14) deals with the attitude of repentant humility required for being right with God, while the two scenes (vv. 15–17; 18–30) emphasize the openness of faith and the absolute commitment to Jesus that is necessary.

18:9 *confident of their own righteousness*. This typifies the attitude of a person who assumes—wrongly—that their performance in life satisfies God's standards (Gal. 3:10–14; Phil. 3:3–9).

looked down on everybody else. Literally, this is "to treat with contempt." The Pharisees considered themselves superior to other Jews who were unable (or unwilling) to conform to their detailed interpretation of the Law of Moses.

> *The parable deals with the attitude of repentant humility required for being right with God.*

18:10 *went up to the temple to pray.* Twice daily, the priests at the temple offered a lamb as a sacrifice of atonement for the sins of the people. At these services, people would gather to join in the liturgy and pray.

Pharisee. The Pharisees were a small, powerful religious sect whose prime concern was keeping the Law in all its detail. While modern readers of the New Testament assume the Pharisees are the "bad guys" in the story, the original audience of this parable respected them as especially devout, godly people.

tax collector. Jesus' listeners would have considered a tax collector as vile as a robber or murderer. Tax collectors were thought to be traitors, because they collaborated with the Roman power in order to become wealthy. Since only the tax collector knew the tax rate required by Rome, he was free to charge whatever the market would bear. Once he paid what he owed Rome, the rest was his to keep.

18:11 *stood up.* This was the typical posture for prayer. The contrast with the position of the tax collector (v. 13) indicates the Pharisee may have stood as closely as possible to the Most Holy Place in the temple, because he assumed the right to draw near to the presence of God.

God, I thank you. To us it is unimaginable that such a prayer might be said in public, yet it would not be unusual for holy men of the time to pray publicly like this. One well-known rabbinic prayer that dates to a time not too long after the time of Jesus reads: "Praised be the Lord that He did not make me a heathen, for all heathen are as nothing before him; praised be He that He did not make me a woman, for woman is not under obligation to fulfill the law; praised be He that He did not make me … an uneducated man, for the uneducated man is not cautious to avoid sins" (Scott). The Pharisee may have felt it his duty to offer such a prayer aloud as a way of instructing "sinners" in the crowd about the way of righteousness.

I am not like other men. In the Talmud, one rabbi was reported to have been so confident of his own righteousness that were only a hundred saved from judgment, he and his son would be among that number; if only two, then he felt that it would be he and his son!

this tax collector. While the NIV separates the listing of robbers, evildoers and adulterers from the tax collector, the grammar of the verse also allows the entire list to be meant as a reference to the tax collector. They were considered robbers and cheats. Adultery might have been added to highlight the tax collector's sinfulness, or may have been meant figuratively to describe someone who has forsaken loyalty to God. The Pharisee's prayer may well be an attack on the very fact that such a man would dare be present in the temple.

18:12 *I fast twice a week.* While Jews were only required to fast on the Day of Atonement, Pharisees fasted every Monday and Thursday in an attempt to gain merit with God. Although all Jews were expected to give a tithe of one's produce, Pharisees carefully tithed even things that were not required (see

Luke 11:42). This man's external performance of religious obligations was exemplary.

18:13 *stood at a distance.* The tax collector likewise stands apart from the crowd, because he is too ashamed to join them.

beat his breast. Bailey points out that this is an uncommon action for a Middle Eastern man, done only on occasions of great anguish.

have mercy. Literally, this is "make an atonement." In light of the ceremony under way at the temple, the tax collector pleads that the atoning sacrifice might apply to him. He realizes this is his only hope before God.

18:14 *I tell you that this man ... went home justified.* Here is where the listeners would have been surprised. How could it be that the Pharisee, the model of righteousness, is not right before God, whereas the tax collector is forgiven, acquitted by God? The surprising twist in the parable is that righteousness is a matter of humble self-recognition of sin and dependence upon the atonement God provides as a gift (rather than a matter of impressing God with one's performance).

For everyone who exalts himself will be humbled, and he who humbles himself will be exalted. This was a common wisdom saying that echoes a central theme in Jewish teaching about the spiritual life (see 1 Sam. 2:8; Ps. 18:27; Prov. 3:34; Isa. 57:15; Matt. 23:12; Luke 1:52; 14:11). The parable simply reminds the listeners of a truth they should have realized long ago.

A Good Man Is Hard to Find

"Consider the characters in this parable. Forget the prejudice that Jesus' frequently stinging remarks about Pharisees have formed in your mind. Give this particular Pharisee all the credit you can. He is, after all, a good man. To begin with, he is not a crook, not a timeserver, not a womanizer. He takes nothing he hasn't honestly earned, he gives everyone he knows fair and full measure, and he is faithful to his wife, patient with his children, and steadfast for his friends. He is not at all like this publican, this tax-farmer, who is the worst kind of crook: a

legal one, a big operator, a mafia-style enforcer working for the Roman government on a nifty franchise that lets him collect—from his fellow Jews, mind you, from the people whom the Romans might have trouble finding, but whose whereabouts he knows and whose language he speaks—all the money he can bleed out of them, provided only he pays the authorities an agreed flat fee. He has been living for years on the cream he has skimmed off their milk money ...

"The Pharisee, however, is not only good; he is religious. And not hypocritically religious, either. His outward uprightness is matched by an inward discipline. He fasts twice a week and he puts his money where his mouth is: ten percent off the top for God. If you know where to find a dozen or two such upstanding citizens, I know several parishes that will accept delivery of them, no questions asked and all Jesus' parables to the contrary notwithstanding.

"But best of all, this Pharisee thanks God for his happy state ...

"Do you see now what Jesus is saying in this parable? He is saying that as far as the Pharisee's ability to win a game of justification with God is concerned, he is no better off than the publican. As a matter of fact, the Pharisee is worse off: because while they're both losers, the publican at least has the sense to recognize the fact and trust God's offer of a free drink. The point of the parable is that they are both dead, and their only hope is someone who can raise the dead.

"We hate this parable because it says plainly that it is the nightmare that is the truth of our condition. We fear the publican's acceptance because we know precisely what it means. It means that we will never be free until we are dead to the whole business of justifying ourselves. But since that business is our life, that means not until we are dead.

"For Jesus came to raise the dead. Not to reform the reformable, not to improve the improvable ... Let us make an end: as long as you are struggling like the Pharisee to be alive in your own eyes—and to the precise degree that your struggles are for what is holy, just, and good—you will resent the apparent indifference to your pains that God shows in making the effortlessness of death the touchstone of your justification. Only when you are finally able, with the publican, to admit that you are dead will you be able to stop balking at grace ..." (*Parables of Grace*, by Robert Farrar Capon, Grand Rapids, MI: Eerdmans, 1988, pp. 179,181,184).

2 Prodigal Son—Luke 15:11–32

THREE-PART AGENDA

ICE-BREAKER
15 Minutes

BIBLE STUDY
30 Minutes

CARING TIME
15–45 Minutes

 LEADER: If there's a new person in your group in this session, start with an ice-breaker (see page M7 in the center section). Then begin the session with a word of prayer. If you have more than seven in your group, see the box about the "Fearless Foursome" on page 4. Count off around the group: "one, two, one, two, etc."—and have the "ones" move quickly to another room for the Bible Study.

TO BEGIN THE BIBLE STUDY TIME
(Choose 1 or 2)

1. How many brothers and sisters do you have? Where do you fall in the birth order of your family?

2. When you were a teenager, were you the "obedient" type or the "wild" type?

3. What's the biggest party or celebration your family has over thrown?

READ SCRIPTURE & DISCUSS
(If you don't have time for all the questions in this section, conclude the Bible Study [30 min.] by answering question #7.)

1. When was the first time you left home? What did you miss the most?

2. If you had been the father in this parable, what would you have said when your son came to you wanting his inheritance early so he could leave home?

3. What made the younger son come "to his senses" (v. 17)? What has served as a "wake-up call" in your life?

The Parable of the Lost Son

[11]Jesus continued: "There was a man who had two sons. [12]The younger one said to his father, 'Father, give me my share of the estate.' So he divided his property between them.

[13]"Not long after that, the younger son got together all he had, set off for a distant country and there squandered his wealth in wild living. [14]After he had spent everything, there was a severe famine in that whole country, and he began to be in need. [15]So he went and hired himself out to a citizen of that country, who sent him to his fields to feed pigs. [16]He longed to fill his stomach with the pods that the pigs were eating, but no one gave him anything.

[17]"When he came to his senses, he said, 'How many of my father's hired men have food to spare, and here I am starving to death! [18]I will set out and go back to my father and say to him: Father, I have sinned against heaven and against you. [19]I am no longer worthy to be called your son; make me like one of your hired men.' [20]So he got up and went to his father.

"But while he was still a long way off, his father saw him and was filled with compassion for him; he ran to his son, threw his arms around him and kissed him.

[21]"The son said to him, 'Father, I have sinned against heaven and against you. I am no longer worthy to be called your son.[a]'

[22]"But the father said to his servants, 'Quick! Bring the best robe and put it on him. Put a ring on his finger and sandals on his feet. [23]Bring the fattened calf and kill it. Let's have a feast and celebrate. [24]For this son of mine was dead and is alive again; he was lost and is found.' So they began to celebrate.

[25]"Meanwhile, the older son was in the field. When he came near the house, he heard music and dancing. [26]So he called one of the servants and asked him what was going on. [27]'Your brother has come,' he replied, 'and your father has killed the fattened calf because he has him back safe and sound.'

[28]"The older brother became angry and refused to go in. So his father went out and pleaded with him. [29]But he answered his father, 'Look! All these years I've been slaving for you and never disobeyed your orders. Yet you never gave me even a young goat so I could celebrate with my friends. [30]But when this son of yours who has squandered your property with prostitutes comes home, you kill the fattened calf for him!'

[31]"'My son,' the father said, 'you are always with me, and everything I have is yours. [32]But we had to celebrate and be glad, because this brother of yours was dead and is alive again; he was lost and is found.' "

[a]21 Some early manuscripts *son. Make me like one of your hired men.*

4. What stages does the younger son go through in this parable?

5. Which person do you most identify with in this parable?

6. What does this parable teach you about God's love?

7. If you compared your spiritual journey to this parable, where are you right now: Never left home? Back home after being away? On the way home? In a distant country? Other?

CARING TIME

(Choose 1 or 2 of these questions before closing in prayer. Be sure to pray for the empty chair.)

1. Who would you like to invite to the next meeting to fill "the empty chair"?

2. If you were to describe the last week of your life in terms of weather, what was it like: Sunny and warm? Cold? Scattered showers? Other? What is the forecast for the coming week?

3. How can the group pray for you this week?

P.S. Add new group members to the Group Directory inside the front cover.

15

Notes—Luke 15:11–32

Summary. Marshall notes that this parable "is ... open to a variety of interpretations, dependent on where the main emphasis is thought to lie." For instance, as the Parable of the Loving Father it illustrates the boundless, lavish love of God toward his wayward children (for Old Testament roots of this truth, see Jer. 3:18–20; 31:18–20). As the Parable of the Lost Son, it shows the process of repentance and the joy that awaits the sinner who will turn to God. As the Parable of the Older Son, it forces the Pharisees to consider the meaning of their own hostility over Jesus' reception of the tax collectors and sinners (Luke 15:1–2).

15:12 _give me my share of the estate._ Under Jewish law, the younger of two sons would receive one-third of the estate upon his father's death (Deut. 21:17). While a father might divide up his property before he died if he wished, this son's request would be considered unbelievably callous and hard-hearted. In essence, he implies that the fact that his father still lives is getting in the way of his plans. The father was under no obligation whatsoever to grant this request; the audience would expect a father faced with such an insulting request to respond with anger. Instead, this father goes along with the request and divides the property between his sons.

15:13 _got together all he had._ In other words, the younger son sold off his share of the estate so that he could have cold, hard cash to do with what he wanted! Such an action would have been scandalous at a time when a person's identity and future was tied up with his family's land. For the sake of satisfying immediate pleasures, he has separated himself from his family, thrown away his means of income, and robbed any children he may have in the future of the security of owning land.

wild living. Elsewhere this term is translated as "debauchery" (Eph. 5:18) or "flood of dissipation" (1 Peter 4:4).

15:15 _hired himself out ... to feed pigs._ Jews considered pigs to be ceremonially unclean animals (Lev. 11:7) and would not eat, raise, or touch them. There was even the pronouncement of a curse upon the person who cared for them (Hendriksen).

15:16 _He longed to fill his stomach with the pods that the pigs were eating._ While eating the food of pigs sounds terrible even to modern readers, for the Pharisees in this audience it would have been utterly horrifying. Jesus has painted a picture of an unbelievably arrogant, unpleasant, immoral, foolish and irreligious young man.

15:17 _he came to his senses._ The phrase does not indicate repentance, but simply a recognition that the way he has chosen is not working. He thus rehearses a speech acknowledging his misdeeds in hopes that his father might receive him back. Bailey points out that at this point the only sin the son may recognize is that by squandering his inheritance, he now has no money with which to care for his father in his old age. His plan to work for his father as a servant may be so that he might be able to at least partially meet that obligation.

15:19 _no longer worthy to be called your son._ The son realized that he had no legal, moral or relational claim on his father's goodwill.

hired men. These were day laborers employed only as the day-to-day work of the estate would happen to demand.

15:20 Just as the actions of the son scandalized the Pharisees, so the response of the father violated their understanding of how such a son should be treated.

his father saw him. The implication is that the father had been waiting and hoping to one day see his son return.

was filled with compassion. There is no haughtiness of wounded pride, but only the welling up of pity, love and joy.

ran to his son. Protocol and dignity is thrown to the wind as the father races to his son. Social customs dictated that it was degrading for an elderly man to run to anyone, especially to someone who had so disgraced him. This picture presents an absolutely unique, staggering insight into the response of the Almighty Holy God to a repentant sinner. Bailey comments that in the village setting of this parable, the villagers would have gathered around when they heard the son was returning in order to taunt him for his foolishness. While the son expected to face running the gauntlet of such taunts, he would have been shocked to see his father welcome him

instead, thus sheltering him from the insults of the townspeople.

kissed him. While this was a typical greeting for men, it would have been thought inappropriate given the son's grave offense against his father.

15:21 ***I am no longer worthy to be called your son.*** Although the son may have thought he could earn his way back into some relationship with his father in order to alleviate his own misery, at this point he reflects a true sense of repentance: He can offer nothing except a contrite spirit (Ps. 51:17).

15:22 The father sets the stage for how the son is to be treated by others.

the best robe. This would have been the father's best robe. This is a sign that people should honor him as they honor the father.

a ring. The signet ring gives the son the authority to represent the father.

sandals. Being shoeless was a sign of a slave. To wear shoes indicated a man was free to go where he pleased. Thus the son is immediately and unconditionally elevated to a position of honor and respect in the home.

15:23 ***fattened calf.*** This was "an animal specially fed and kept to be slaughtered on a special occasion" (Marshall). The fact that it was a calf that was prepared indicates that the whole village was invited to come to the feast (for such provisions could feed 100 people). Bailey notes that when an animal was slaughtered for a feast for a special guest, its blood was sprinkled on the threshold of the home. Stepping over the blood into the home was a sign of a covenant between guest and host. In this case, it would indicate a new covenant of love between the father and his son.

15:24 ***was dead.*** It was as if the son were dead (in the sense that he apparently had no intention to live in relationship with his father ever again).

15:25–32 The focus of the parable shifts to the older son (who represents the Pharisees).

15:28 This son was furious at the treatment his younger brother received. He could only see that the father had violated all the customs of how such a wayward son should be treated. His refusal to enter the house would have been seen as a sign of grave disrespect, since the eldest son was expected to play the part of a gracious host at a family feast. As he did with the younger son, the father "went out" to "plead with" the older son. This too was an overwhelming display of grace, since his son's refusal to come to the party was a serious social insult. The parable's listeners would have expected the father to be enraged.

15:29 While the father's love wrought humility in the younger son, the older son responds with even more insulting behavior.

Look! This would have been considered an extremely rude way for a son to address his father, since there is no hint of respect or affection.

I've been slaving for you. Ironically, this son views his ongoing relationship with his father in the way the younger son hoped he might be privileged to have. While always in the vicinity of the father, the older son never enjoyed the relationship with his father that was available to him.

never disobeyed your orders. While there was the appearance of cooperation with the father, this son apparently always viewed things in terms of a master/slave relationship. This reflected the Pharisees' reliance upon external conformity to God's Law as the measure by which one could eventually earn his blessing.

you never gave me. This observation ignores that he has always been in the position to enjoy the love of his father, whereas the younger son has not.

15:31 ***everything I have is yours.*** This would assure the older son that he is in no danger of losing his inheritance because of the presence of his younger brother. The father does not see his older son as a servant, but as an heir. He, too, should celebrate at his brother's homecoming. We are not told what the older son did. Jesus purposely left the story open-ended to force the Pharisees (and modern readers) to fill in the ending by their behavior.

3 The Sower—Mark 4:1–20

THREE-PART AGENDA

ICE-BREAKER	BIBLE STUDY	CARING TIME
15 Minutes	30 Minutes	15–45 Minutes

> ☕ **LEADER:** *Remember to choose an appropriate ice-breaker if you have a new person at the meeting (see page M7 in the center section), and then begin with a prayer. If you have more than seven in your group, divide into groups of four for the Bible Study (see the box about the "Fearless Foursome" on page 4).*

TO BEGIN THE BIBLE STUDY TIME
(Choose 1 or 2)

1. How "green" is your thumb? Who do you know that can make anything grow?

2. What teacher have you appreciated for taking the time to help you understand something?

3. What has been your biggest worry lately?

READ SCRIPTURE & DISCUSS
(If you don't have time for all the questions in this section, conclude the Bible Study [30 min.] by answering question #7.)

1. When do you recall someone planting the "seed" of the Gospel in your life?

2. According to Jesus, why does God's Word not take root at all in some people (v. 15)? What causes the plants in the second type of soil to wither (vv. 16–17)? What three things choked off the third plants (vv. 18–19)?

3. What do you think Jesus means by the spectacular harvest produced by the good soil (v. 20): New converts? Good deeds? Godly character qualities?

The Parable of the Sower

4 *Again Jesus began to teach by the lake. The crowd that gathered around him was so large that he got into a boat and sat in it out on the lake, while all the people were along the shore at the water's edge. ²He taught them many things by parables, and in his teaching said: ³"Listen! A farmer went out to sow his seed. ⁴As he was scattering the seed, some fell along the path, and the birds came and ate it up. ⁵Some fell on rocky places, where it did not have much soil. It sprang up quickly, because the soil was shallow. ⁶But when the sun came up, the plants were scorched, and they withered because they had no root. ⁷Other seed fell among thorns, which grew up and choked the plants, so that they did not bear grain. ⁸Still other seed fell on good soil. It came up, grew and produced a crop, multiplying thirty, sixty, or even a hundred times."*

⁹Then Jesus said, "He who has ears to hear, let him hear."

¹⁰When he was alone, the Twelve and the others around him asked him about the parables. ¹¹He told them, "The secret of the kingdom of God has been given to you. But to those on the outside everything is said in parables ¹²so that,

" 'they may be ever seeing but never perceiving, and ever hearing but never understanding; otherwise they might turn and be forgiven!'ᵃ"

¹³Then Jesus said to them, "Don't you understand this parable? How then will you understand any parable? ¹⁴The farmer sows the word. ¹⁵Some people are like seed along the path, where the word is sown. As soon as they hear it, Satan comes and takes away the word that was sown in them. ¹⁶Others, like seed sown on rocky places, hear the word and at once receive it with joy. ¹⁷But since they have no root, they last only a short time. When trouble or persecution comes because of the word, they quickly fall away. ¹⁸Still others, like seed sown among thorns, hear the word; ¹⁹but the worries of this life, the deceitfulness of wealth and the desires for other things come in and choke the word, making it unfruitful. ²⁰Others, like seed sown on good soil, hear the word, accept it, and produce a crop—thirty, sixty or even a hundred times what was sown."

ᵃ *12* Isaiah 6:9,10

4. How satisfied are you with the time and energy you give to hearing and acting on God's Word?

5. Which of the four kinds of soil best describes the condition of your heart right now?

6. What in your life provides nutrients to your soil? What are the "thorns" and "rocks" that tend to choke your spiritual growth?

7. What can you do to develop stronger spiritual roots?

CARING TIME
(Choose 1 or 2 of these questions before closing in prayer. Be sure to pray for the empty chair.)

1. How do you feel about sharing your needs and struggles with this group?

2. Does every person in the group have a position on the team roster (review p. M5)?

3. How can the group help you in prayer this week?

Notes—Mark 4:1–20

Summary. The emphasis in the so-called Parable of the Sower is really on the soils. The parable fits into the context of Mark's Gospel. The four soils represent the four kinds of responses to Jesus seen thus far in the Gospel. They also foreshadow the kinds of responses that are to come later on in the story. It can also be helpful to consider the parable (vv. 3–8) by itself in order to find what else Jesus might have been implying about the kingdom through the story. For instance, what does it imply about proclaiming the message? What does it indicate about the ultimate result of such proclamation? What does it imply about the effectiveness of the "word" despite the hardships it might encounter?

4:2 *parables.* Parables are comparisons which draw upon common experiences in order to teach about kingdom realities. These metaphors or analogies draw upon the known to force the hearer to consider the reality of the unknown.

4:3 *sow his seed.* Farmers would throw seed into the soil by a broadcast method. While many commentators maintain that Palestinian farmers sowed their seeds first, indiscriminately throwing seed throughout the entire plot before plowing the ground (including the areas with weeds and a rocky base under shallow soil), others assert that the only real evidence for such an odd practice is this parable! The latter think that the indiscriminate sowing of this particular farmer was one of the strange twists that would have captured the attention of Jesus' hearers as they would have immediately asked themselves, "Why would the farmer throw seed into an area where there are weeds or rocks?"

4:4 *the path.* There were long, hard pathways between the various plots of land. The soil was so packed down that seed could not penetrate the soil and germinate. The birds came along and ate up this seed which just sat on the surface of the ground.

4:5 *rocky places.* Some of the soil covered a limestone base a few inches beneath the surface. Seed that fell here would germinate, but it would not last (since a proper root system could not develop because of the rock).

4:7 *thorns.* In other parts of the plot there were the roots of weeds. As the seed grew up, so did the weeds (which invariably stunted the growth of the good seed). Although it lived, such seed would not bear fruit.

4:8 *good soil.* However, some of the seed fell where it was intended.

thirty, sixty, or even a hundred times. The good soil yielded a spectacular crop. The normal yield for a Palestinian field is seven and a half times what is sown, while 10 times is an especially good harvest. This is where the emphasis in the parable lies: not with the unproductive soil but with the miracle crop.

4:9 Jesus urges his hearers to ponder his parable. Part of the power of a parable lies in the fact that people must reflect on it in order to understand it. To grasp the meaning of a parable, people must have the key to it. They must know the subject that the parable is about. So the question is, "What topic does this story from ordinary life provide insight into?"

let him hear. The concept of spiritual deafness is an important theme in the Gospel of Mark. The crowds are deaf to the meaning of Jesus' words, as are the teachers of the Law (and even the disciples). Jesus twice heals deaf people, and for Mark this act is symbolic of the healing that must go on for all people (in this case, the Twelve) in order for them to understand who Jesus really is (see Mark 4:12,23; 7:31–37; 8:18; 9:14–32).

4:10 The subject of Jesus' parables is not yet clear—even to the disciples! Nor in fact will his teaching become fully clear to the disciples before his death. It is not easy for them (and others) to question their assumptions about the way God works in order to see who Jesus really is and what the kingdom is actually all about.

4:11–12 At first reading, this may appear to be saying that parables are designed to obscure the truth. This simply states (with some irony) what is a fact: some respond to Jesus and some do not. The teachers of the Law, for example, see Jesus' miracles and hear his teaching, yet they ascribe his power to Satan (Mark 3:22). They see but do not perceive.

4:11 *The secret.* A secret in the New Testament is not something which is hidden; rather, it is something which was previously unknown but has now been revealed to all who will hear. The secret given the disciples is that the kingdom of God has come.

the kingdom of God. How God establishes his reign in human affairs is what Jesus' parables in this section are all about. This is the interpretive key.

has been given you. Not even the disciples (who have been given "the secret") perceive fully what is going on (v. 13). To be "given the secret" means something like "called to follow Jesus." It is as the disciples follow Jesus that they will come to understand more fully what he means.

those on the outside. The point is not that God calls some and excludes others. Rather, those who are on the outside are simply those who fail to pursue the kingdom. The secret is open to all who, like the disciples, ask.

4:12 ever seeing / ever hearing. This quote is from Isaiah 6:9–10 (in which God called the prophet to speak his word, even though Israel would not listen). Although they saw God's messenger and heard his word, they refused to heed his message.

otherwise they might turn and be forgiven. It was not that God did not want people to repent as a result of the preaching of Isaiah. This verse can only be understood when one sees it as full of irony, a characteristic of Isaiah's writing. From God's perspective, the behavior of the people is such that it seems the last thing they want to do is actually experience God's forgiveness. Choosing rather to persist in sin, they cover their eyes and block their ears to God's word so that they will not be persuaded to turn to God. Jesus uses this quote to indicate the same thing is happening in his day. Those on the outside are those who refuse to see and hear what he is saying because they do not want to change their ways.

4:13–20 This is the only parable interpreted in this Gospel. This fact, coupled with its length (20 verses, when most stories occupy 10 verses or less) indicates how important this parable is for Mark in the telling of his story. By it, Mark helps the reader understand the four types of responses to Jesus seen thus far in the Gospel. From Mark 3:7–35, it would appear that two responses to Jesus are negative (the teachers of the Law and the family) and two positive (the crowds and the Twelve). But here in this parable it becomes clear that only one response (that of the Twelve) will bear fruit for the kingdom.

4:14 The seed is the message of God's kingdom.

4:15 Some, like the teachers of the Law, are so hardened (like the soil on the paths between plots) that the seed of the word never penetrates. It is snatched away by Satan before it can germinate.

Satan. The teachers of the Law have charged Jesus with being dominated by Satan. However, it turns out that they are the ones under his influence!

4:16–17 Others, like the crowds, are superficially attracted to Jesus. They like what he can give them (powerful teaching, healing of disease, casting out of demons), but the level of their commitment is not deep. It will fall away as soon as there is any hint of persecution.

receive it with joy. Indeed, the common people flocked to Jesus once they saw what he could do (see Mark 1:16–45; 3:7–12).

4:18–19 Still others, like his family, allow the wrong concerns (Is he eating properly? What gives him the right to fancy himself a rabbi?) to squeeze out the newly growing plant (see Mark 3:20–21,31–35; 6:1–6).

the deceitfulness of wealth and the desires for other things. Following Jesus requires wholehearted loyalty to him. While money and the "other things" in view here are not evil in themselves, the disciple is warned not to allow anything else to take priority over hearing and practicing Jesus' words.

making it unfruitful. The weeds do not kill the plant (unlike the seed sown on hard ground or on rocky soil, neither of which survive), but they do not allow it to bring forth fruit.

4:20 But in the end, some, like the Twelve, will produce abundant fruit (see Mark 3:13–19).

a crop. The crop in view is a life full of the qualities of discipleship, such as righteousness, love, joy, peace, goodness, etc. (Gal. 5:22–23; Phil. 1:11).

thirty, sixty or even a hundred times. While it may appear there are three types of unproductive soil (hard, rocky, weed–filled) and three types of productive soil (that bearing thirty–fold, that bearing sixty–fold, and that bearing a hundred–fold), in essence the point is that there are only two kinds of soil: unproductive and productive.

4 Unmerciful Servant—Matt. 18:21–35

THREE-PART AGENDA

ICE-BREAKER
15 Minutes

BIBLE STUDY
30 Minutes

CARING TIME
15–45 Minutes

> *LEADER: If there's a new person in this session, start with an ice-breaker from the center section (see page M7). Remember to stick closely to the three-part agenda and the time allowed for each segment. Is your group praying for the empty chair?*

TO BEGIN THE BIBLE STUDY TIME
(Choose 1 or 2)

1. Growing up, were you more likely to "pick on" others or be picked on by others?

2. What is one debt you were extremely relieved to have paid off?

3. To whom do you have to say "I'm sorry" to the most often: Parents? Kids? Friends? Boss? Coworkers? Spouse? Siblings? Neighbors? Other?

READ SCRIPTURE & DISCUSS
(If you don't have time for all the questions in this section, conclude the Bible Study [30 min.] by answering question #7.)

1. Do you tend to be quick or slow to forgive?

2. How do you feel about Jesus' answer (v. 22) to Peter's question (v. 21)? What is Jesus really saying?

3. What is the comparison between the two servants' debts (vv. 24,28)? Their pleas (vv. 26,29)? The decision about their case (vv. 27,30)?

The Parable of the Unmerciful Servant

21 Then Peter came to Jesus and asked, "Lord, how many times shall I forgive my brother when he sins against me? Up to seven times?"

*22 Jesus answered, "I tell you, not seven times, but seventy-seven times.*a

*23 "Therefore, the kingdom of heaven is like a king who wanted to settle accounts with his servants. 24 As he began the settlement, a man who owed him ten thousand talents*b *was brought to him. 25 Since he was not able to pay, the master ordered that he and his wife and his children and all that he had be sold to repay the debt.*

26 "The servant fell on his knees before him. 'Be patient with me,' he begged, 'and I will pay back everything.' 27 The servant's master took pity on him, canceled the debt and let him go.

*28 "But when that servant went out, he found one of his fellow servants who owed him a hundred denarii.*c *He grabbed him and began to choke him. 'Pay back what you owe me!' he demanded.*

29 "His fellow servant fell to his knees and begged him, 'Be patient with me, and I will pay you back.'

30 "But he refused. Instead, he went off and had the man thrown into prison until he could pay the debt. 31 When the other servants saw what had happened, they were greatly distressed and went and told their master everything that had happened.

32 "Then the master called the servant in. 'You wicked servant,' he said, 'I canceled all that debt of yours because you begged me to. 33 Shouldn't you have had mercy on your fellow servant just as I had on you?' 34 In anger his master turned him over to the jailers to be tortured, until he should pay back all he owed.

35 "This is how my heavenly Father will treat each of you unless you forgive your brother from your heart."

a*22 Or seventy times seven*　　b*24 That is, millions of dollars*
c*28 That is, a few dollars*

4. If you were the master, how would you have felt when the servant refused to forgive a fellow servant's debt—right after you had forgiven his huge debt?

5. Which character in this parable can you most relate to and why?

6. What have you found helpful in forgiving those who have wronged you?

7. How has God's forgiveness affected your life and your willingness to forgive?

CARING TIME

(Choose 1 or 2 of these questions before closing in prayer. Be sure to pray for the empty chair.)

1. How would you describe your relationship with God right now: Close? Distant? Improving? Strained? Other?

2. How are you doing at inviting others to the group? Who could you invite for next week?

3. How can the group support you in prayer this week?

Notes—Matthew 18:21-35

Summary. Matthew 18:15–20 introduces the topic of sin, forgiveness and reconciliation. Here, this discussion is continued in order to get at the heart of the reason why the disciple of Jesus is to be merciful and forgiving toward others.

18:21 *how many times shall I forgive my brother when he sins against me? Up to seven times?* The rabbis taught that a person ought to be forgiven for a particular offense up to three times. After that, the offended person was under no obligation to grant forgiveness. Realizing that Jesus had a greater sense of the importance of mercy than was typical for rabbis, Peter was willing to double the traditional amount plus add one more time for good measure! Since seven was considered the number of completion and perfection, Peter may have thought that anyone who could forgive someone that many times would be a spiritually perfect person.

18:22 *seventy-seven times.* This could also be understood as seventy times seven. Whichever reading is correct, by taking what Peter thought was a generous offer and multiplying it in this way, Jesus explodes any notion of a limit to forgiveness! It is probable that "seventy-seven" is the correct reading, since it is the same number found in the Greek version of Genesis 4:24 (which refers to a comment made by Lamech, a violent man and descendant from Cain, the first murderer). After Cain's murder of Abel, God placed a curse upon him but assured him that anyone who harmed him would suffer vengeance seven times over (Gen. 4:15). Lamech, five generations later, twisted God's promise of mercy to Cain into a boastful threat that if anyone tried to harm him for his murder of another man, then vengeance would be taken seventy-seven times over. Jesus took what was a pattern for ever-increasing vengeance and transformed it to one of ever-increasing forgiveness.

18:23–34 To illustrate the need for forgiveness of others, Matthew includes this parable. While it does not directly relate to the concern of Peter (about the number of times one ought to forgive someone), it does get to the heart of the matter regarding why the lack of forgiveness is inexcusable for a disciple of Jesus.

18:23–27 Act One of the parable introduces the reader to a king and a servant with a tremendous debt.

18:23 *a king.* Given the amount of money involved and the form of punishment, it is clear that the "king" in view here is no ancient Jewish king. Rather, Jesus is tapping the people's imagination of what the fabulously wealthy kings of Egypt or Persia must have been like.

settle accounts. Kings would entrust the day-to-day affairs of their kingdom to the management of servants (who were responsible for pursuing the king's best interest in their responsibilities). Such a servant might have been the manager of several tax stations responsible for collecting revenue for the king. This was an audit to check on how the servants were doing with respect to their management.

18:24 *ten thousand talents.* This is difficult to translate into an exact modern-day amount. However, the point is that it is an impossibly high amount, as if a person today was found to be millions (or even billions) of dollars in debt. Herod the Great, who ruled over Palestine at the time of Jesus' birth, had an annual tax revenue of only about 900 talents. The crowd listening to Jesus would have gasped at the thought of having to pay someone such a fantastically high amount of money.

18:25 *he and his wife and his children and all that he had be sold.* Jewish kings could not do this, but "The oriental king was all powerful, possessing the right of life and death over his subjects" (Hill). Thus, the king had the right to divide up the man's family to sell them into slavery to recoup at least a fraction of his losses.

18:26 *I will pay back everything.* This was an impossible promise. While it may reflect his sincere desire to save himself and his family, it was beyond his ability to carry out.

18:27 This verse reflects the heart, not only of the king, but of God. The king's actions would have been totally unexpected (given the popular image of cruel, powerful, heartless kings). Instead, here is

one who forgave a lowly servant for no reason! The king gained nothing for this action. The twist of the parable at this point is that kings aren't supposed to act like this!

took pity. Elsewhere in Matthew, this same word, translated as "compassion," is used to describe the attitude of Jesus toward the sick (9:36), toward the hungry (15:32), and toward the blind (20:34). Like the man in this story, none of the people Jesus had compassion for were able to do anything about their situation.

canceled the debt. For readers familiar with the meaning of Jesus' death, this allusion to what God has done for sinners in Christ would be inescapable. The New Testament sometimes pictures sin as a debt owed to God that has been canceled because of God's mercy in Christ (Rom. 6:23; Col. 2:13–15).

and let him go. The man was free. The impossible burden that must have crushed him with fear (while he wondered what would happen to him when his mismanagement was discovered) was suddenly gone. There was no debt-restructuring that would still keep him indebted to the king for the rest of his life. There was no alternative form of punishment. The enormous losses he had created for the king were simply forgiven. He could start life over again without this terrible burden upon him (see Rom. 8:1–2).

18:28–30 This is Act Two. The first servant meets another man who owes him some money. While the reader leaves Act One rejoicing with the servant, Act Two reveals how repulsive he truly is.

18:28 *a hundred denarii.* Since a denarii was a day's wage for a laborer, this is a reasonably large amount. However, it pales into insignificance when compared to the sum the first servant owed the king (at the rate of one denarius a day, it would have taken 15 years of earnings just to pay back a single talent!).

18:29 In words similar to what the first servant had spoken to the king, the second servant promises to repay the debt. In the case of the first servant, such a promise was impossible; in this case repayment could easily have been made over time. The first

servant did not need to cancel the debt as had the king; he could have given the second servant some more time.

18:30 *But he refused.* This is the second surprise twist in the parable. Under the circumstances, this man would have been expected to forego the debt. Instead, he insists on carrying out the full weight of the law against the servant indebted to him. The mercy he has received from the king has not produced any new sense of moral character in this man. Instead, he still wants to operate on terms of strict justice.

> *Christ's disciples are obligated to forgive others continually.*

thrown into prison. In a debtor's prison, the man's assets would have to be sold in order to make payment.

18:31–34 In Act Three, the king is told of the situation and responds in anger. The readers would be in sympathy with the others who told the king about the actions of the first servant. He has violated the mercy of the king by refusing to extend mercy to the second servant. No one would doubt that now his punishment is justly deserved.

18:33 *Shouldn't you have had mercy ... just as I had on you?* This is the point of the parable. As recipients of mercy from God, Christ's disciples are obligated to forgive others continually. Not to do so is as incongruous as is the action of the servant in the story. Not to do so is to reveal that they have not grasped the reality of the mercy they have received from God.

18:34 *to be tortured.* The man will now be pressed for every cent he has.

18:35 The parable is applied to the listeners: As in Matthew 6:14–15, God's forgiveness of us is to shape the way we forgive others. If it does not, we remain under judgment. Thus, Matthew emphasizes the need for the Christian community to be a place where forgiveness is found in abundant supply.

5 Good Samaritan—Luke 10:25–37

THREE-PART AGENDA

ICE-BREAKER
15 Minutes

BIBLE STUDY
30 Minutes

CARING TIME
15–45 Minutes

> **LEADER:** *If there's a new person in this session, start with an ice-breaker from the center section (see page M7). Remember to stick closely to the three-part agenda and the time allowed for each segment. Is your group praying for the empty chair? As the leader, you may want to choose question #1 in the Caring Time to facilitate the group in handling accountability issues.*

TO BEGIN THE BIBLE STUDY TIME
(Choose 1 or 2)

1. When have you been stranded on the side of the road? Who came to your rescue?

2. Growing up, what neighbor were you closest to? Who is your closest neighbor now?

3. What's the closest you've come to being mugged or robbed?

READ SCRIPTURE & DISCUSS
(If you don't have time for all the questions in this section, conclude the Bible Study [30 min.] by answering question #7.)

1. Who would you nominate for the "Good Samaritan Award" in your neighborhood, church or this group?

2. If you had been traveling down the road to Jericho and saw the hurt man, what would you have likely done?

3. What may be some reasons the priest and Levite didn't stop to help the hurt man?

The Parable of the Good Samaritan

²⁵On one occasion an expert in the law stood up to test Jesus. "Teacher," he asked, "what must I do to inherit eternal life?"

²⁶"What is written in the Law?" he replied. "How do you read it?"

²⁷He answered: " 'Love the Lord your God with all your heart and with all your soul and with all your strength and with all your mind'ᵃ; and, 'Love your neighbor as yourself.'ᵇ"

²⁸"You have answered correctly," Jesus replied. "Do this and you will live."

²⁹But he wanted to justify himself, so he asked Jesus, "And who is my neighbor?"

³⁰In reply Jesus said: "A man was going down from Jerusalem to Jericho, when he fell into the hands of robbers. They stripped him of his clothes, beat him and went away, leaving him half dead. ³¹A priest happened to be going down the same road, and when he saw the man, he passed by on the other side. ³²So too, a Levite, when he came to the place and saw him, passed by on the other side. ³³But a Samaritan, as he traveled, came where the man was; and when he saw him, he took pity on him. ³⁴He went to him and bandaged his wounds, pouring on oil and wine. Then he put the man on his own donkey, took him to an inn and took care of him. ³⁵The next day he took out two silver coinsᶜ and gave them to the innkeeper. 'Look after him,' he said, 'and when I return, I will reimburse you for any extra expense you may have.'

³⁶"Which of these three do you think was a neighbor to the man who fell into the hands of robbers?"

³⁷The expert in the law replied, "The one who had mercy on him."

Jesus told him, "Go and do likewise."

ᵃ*27 Deut. 6:5*   ᵇ*27 Lev. 19:18*   ᶜ*35 Greek two denarii*

4. What reaction would the Jewish listeners have had to Jesus casting a Samaritan as the hero of the story (see note on v. 33)?

5. How does this parable answer the question, "And who is my neighbor" (v. 29)?

6. What grade would you give yourself over this last week for loving God wholeheartedly? For loving others?

7. How can you or this group be a Good Samaritan to someone in need?

CARING TIME
(Choose 1 or 2 of these questions before closing in prayer. Be sure to pray for the empty chair.)

1. For what would you like this group to help hold you accountable?

2. What is something for which you are particularly thankful?

3. How can the group remember you in prayer this week?

Summary. This well-known story is found only in Luke's Gospel. In it Jesus points out how the Jewish leaders, who knew the Law perfectly well, failed to live by it (because of their lack of love for others outside of their own circle).

10:25 an expert in the law. The experts in the Torah were charged with the responsibility of interpreting the Law and teaching people what was involved in its observance.

to test Jesus. The respected theologian was checking out just how astute this young, uncertified teacher really was. His question is meant to force Jesus to penetrate into the heart of the multitudinous commandments that made up Jewish tradition: What is the essential command?

what must I do to inherit eternal life? The rabbis taught that eternal life was gained through the keeping of God's Law, often enumerating various actions that one should follow. The scribe was undoubtedly expecting some such list of requirements that would allow him a basis on which to debate Jesus. Jesus had a reputation among the scribes as one who did not take the Law seriously enough. This would be a chance to trip him up.

10:26 Jesus is not simply returning the question, but is actually answering the lawyer by responding, in essence, "The answer to that is found in what you read of the Law every week in worship. What is that you recite?" This would point the lawyer back to the Shema (Deut. 6:5), which is recited in verse 27. The lawyer combines this with Leviticus 19:18, which stresses the love of one's neighbor. This combination of texts is found in at least one other rabbinic source, indicating it may have been a common way of summarizing the Law.

10:28 Jesus commends the answer. To live in love is the whole meaning of life in the kingdom of God. "The verb 'do' is a present imperative meaning 'keep on doing.' The lawyer requested definition of a specific limited requirement—'what having done I will inherit ...' The answer is given in a command for an open-ended lifestyle that requires unlimited and unqualified love for God and people" (Bailey).

10:29 The lawyer senses that he is being tested rather than Jesus (v. 25)! In an attempt to regain the initiative and transform this encounter into a debate about what the Law means by "neighbor," he asks Jesus another question. Given the understanding of "neighbor" at the time, his follow-up question was perfectly natural. For instance, the Pharisees assumed only other Pharisees were their neighbors, while other sects within Judaism taught that only members of their particular sect were neighbors. Jesus has already pointed out the superficiality of such an interpretation (Luke 6:27–36).

10:30 going down. This "was a notoriously dangerous road ... of narrow, rocky defiles, and of sudden turnings which made it the happy hunting ground of brigands" (Barclay). Roving gangs would ambush people, sometimes by having one gang member pretend to be injured. The road has a reputation of being dangerous for travelers even today.

They stripped him. This detail is important. Since various ethnic groups wore distinctive clothing, it would now be impossible to tell whether the man was a Jew or not.

10:31 A priest. This priest may have been returning home after his period of temple service since Jericho was a principal area where priests lived when not on duty. There are at least two reasons why he may have passed by: (1) He could have thought the man was a sinner; if he helped him he would be working against his just punishment from God; (2) As a priest, he would not want to defile himself by touching a Gentile or a dead man (or even getting within about six feet of the man). Such defilement would be a humiliation after just completing his service at the temple. Defilement was seen as a threat to one's own spiritual condition. The priest's rule-book approach to the spiritual life offered him several compelling reasons why he should simply pass by. He could even consider that he was honoring God by doing so.

10:32 a Levite. These were men assigned to aid the priests in various temple duties. Levites were not under the same regulations that guided the priests, and it appears he may have stopped and looked at the wounded man, perhaps speaking to him. Since he could not identify the man as a neighbor (i.e., a Jew) he, like the priest, decided not to get involved.

10:33 a Samaritan. The introduction of this character would have caught the audience off guard.

Typically, when a person wanted to contrast the pre-occupation of the religious elite over the details of the Law with the "common sense" piety of the average person, the progression would be between "a priest, a Levite, and a Jew," all of whom would have been returning home from service at the temple. Because this was such a stock formula in Jesus' day, the audience would have anticipated that the third man on the scene would be a Jewish layman who would do the right thing. Instead, Jesus invites the scorn of his listeners by this radical alteration of the formula by introducing a "good" Samaritan into the story. It would be like telling the story of "The Good Palestinian" to present-day Jews in Israel or the story of "The Good Apache" to residents of a western U.S. town in the 1800s. By making a hero out of a despised person, Jesus puts his Jewish audience in an awkward position: as they consider where they fit in the story, they don't want to identify with the priest and Levite (who showed such callousness), but are they willing to identify with a Samaritan? While priests and Levites had distinguished places in Jewish society, Samaritans were despised as half-breeds who had blended the worship of God with pagan practices. This term was used as an insult to describe a Jew who did not pay strict enough attention to religious tradition (John 8:48). While the roots of this prejudice reached back to the conquest of the northern kingdom of Israel by the Assyrians in 722 B.C., this ancient animosity was fresh in Jesus' day because some Samaritans had recently defiled the temple in Jerusalem by scattering bones in it. Prayers were offered daily that Samaritans might not be given eternal life.

took pity on him. Unlike the priest and Levite, the Samaritan was moved by compassion and stopped to help. Of all the characters in the story so far, he would have the least reason to suspect that the wounded man was his neighbor (i.e., a fellow Samaritan). Nevertheless, he helped him simply because he was a man in need.

> *"The question is not, 'Who is my neighbor?' but 'Am I being a neighbor to those needy ones whom the Lord places in my path?' "*

10:34 ***bandaged his wounds.*** Bailey notes that this phrase, as well as many details in the story, is a strong allusion to Hosea 6:1–10, which describes how God will "bind up (the) wounds" of rebellious Israel. The Samaritan is not only the hero of the story, he becomes a God-figure!

pouring on oil and wine. While olive oil and wine were thought to have medicinal benefits, they were also used in acts of worship at the temple. The implication is that this use of the wine and oil represents true worship of God.

took him to an inn. The nearest inn would be in Jericho, a place where Samaritans would be unwelcome. For the Samaritan to be willing to be identified was an act of love and courage, since the Jews in the community around the inn would assume that the Samaritan was somehow responsible for the injury to their tribesman.

10:35 ***two silver coins.*** Literally, this is two denarii, enough to care for the man for three weeks. The Samaritan also promised to reimburse whatever else it might cost to care for the man. Whereas the robbers beat, robbed and left the man, the Samaritan bound up his wounds, brought him to safety, and promised to return.

10:36 ***Which ... was a neighbor ...?*** Jesus rephrases the lawyer's question (v. 29). Rather than join the game of defining who is (and, therefore, who is not) one's neighbor, he points out to this Jewish lawyer that he should act at least as generously and neighborly as this Samaritan (who had absolutely no ethnic or social obligation to the wounded man). "The question is not, 'Who is my neighbor?' but 'Am I being a neighbor to those needy ones whom the Lord places in my path?' " (Hendriksen). It is such sacrificial, generous, and reckless love that is the evidence of truly loving God and others, and thus of the assurance of eternal life (v. 25).

6 Rich Fool—Luke 12:13–21

THREE-PART AGENDA

ICE-BREAKER
15 Minutes

BIBLE STUDY
30 Minutes

CARING TIME
15–45 Minutes

> *LEADER: Check page M7 in the center section for a good ice-breaker, particularly if you have a new person at this meeting. Is your group working well together—with everyone "fielding their position" as shown on the team roster on page M5?*

TO BEGIN THE BIBLE STUDY TIME
(Choose 1 or 2)

1. What did you like to collect as a kid? What do you like to collect now?

2. What family heirloom would you like to someday inherit?

3. What would the "dream" retirement situation be for you?

READ SCRIPTURE & DISCUSS
(If you don't have time for all the questions in this section, conclude the Bible Study [30 min.] by answering question #7.)

1. When it comes to saving for the future, how do you determine how much is "enough"?

2. What was Jesus warning against in verse 15 when he said, "Watch out!"?

3. What problem did the man in this parable face? What was his solution? Why did this displease God?

4. If you had been in this man's shoes, how would you have solved the problem?

The Parable of the Rich Fool

¹³Someone in the crowd said to him, "Teacher, tell my brother to divide the inheritance with me."

¹⁴Jesus replied, "Man, who appointed me a judge or an arbiter between you?" ¹⁵Then he said to them, "Watch out! Be on your guard against all kinds of greed; a man's life does not consist in the abundance of his possessions."

¹⁶And he told them this parable: "The ground of a certain rich man produced a good crop. ¹⁷He thought to himself, 'What shall I do? I have no place to store my crops.'

¹⁸"Then he said, 'This is what I'll do. I will tear down my barns and build bigger ones, and there I will store all my grain and my goods. ¹⁹And I'll say to myself, "You have plenty of good things laid up for many years. Take life easy; eat, drink and be merry." '

²⁰"But God said to him, 'You fool! This very night your life will be demanded from you. Then who will get what you have prepared for yourself?'

²¹"This is how it will be with anyone who stores up things for himself but is not rich toward God."

5. How pervasive is the attitude, "Take life easy; eat, drink and be merry" (v. 19) in our society? How can this attitude affect your relationship with God?

6. In what way can you be "rich toward God" (v. 21)?

7. What is the lesson for you from this parable?

CARING TIME
(Choose 1 or 2 of these questions before closing in prayer. Be sure to pray for the empty chair.)

1. How is the group doing with its "team assignments" (review the team roster on p. M5)?

2. Rate this past week on a scale of 1 (terrible) to 10 (great). What's the outlook for this week?

3. How would you like the group to pray for you this week?

Notes—Luke 12:13–21

Summary. Whereas the preceding section (Luke 12:1–12) warned the disciples to "be on your guard" against the danger of hypocrisy, this parable warns them to "watch out" (v. 15) for the danger of placing top priority on the concern for material wealth.

12:13 Teacher. Literally, this is "Rabbi." As men schooled in the Law of God, rabbis were often asked to settle legal disputes.

divide the inheritance. When a father died, he would bequeath his estate to his sons in the hope that they might keep the property together. However, if the sons could not "live together in unity" (Ps. 133:1), one could sue for the property to be legally divided. Apparently this man and his brother disagreed about if (or how) such a division should be made.

12:14 Man. This is akin to someone today saying, "Listen, mister ... ." Jesus is clearly rebuking the man for his request.

who appointed me a judge ... between you? Jesus refuses to be used as a pawn for this man's material gain. Instead of being drawn into siding with him as a judge against his brother, Jesus effectively becomes the judge over both of them, exposing the motivation of their hearts. While the man claimed to simply want justice, his vision of justice was more tied up with gaining his share of material possessions than it was with pursuing reconciliation with an estranged brother. The use of "justice" as a cloak for material gain was of no interest to Jesus.

12:15 greed. Jesus pinpoints the real motivating factor behind this appeal for justice. Literally, the word means to "always thirst for more."

life. The Greek word used here (zoe) refers not simply to biological life, but to the quality of one's life. Then, as now, a person's happiness and well-being was often thought to be determined by what they owned. Jesus flatly rejects this as a standard for measuring the worth of one's life.

12:16–20 This parable illustrates the principle of verse 15. Verses 16–17 raise the problem the man faces.

12:16 The ground. The Greek word here, chora, implies "extensive holdings, normally a district or

region" (Scott). The use of this word accentuates the extent of the man's wealth. The fact that this crop was produced by the man's land indicates that the crop was a gift to him. It was not something he particularly earned or deserved. He simply inherited the lavish abundance of a God-given crop.

a good crop. This word is used only here in the New Testament. In the Greek, there is a play on words as the parable develops. The man has an euphoreo ("good crop") which he thinks will lead to euphron ("the enjoyment of the good life"—v. 19), yet God calls him an aphron ("a fool"—v. 20).

12:17 He thought to himself. Kenneth Bailey points out that this is an unusual development for a Middle Eastern man. Typically, such a decision would be a matter of discussion with the other men of the village (who would talk for hours about one another's needs and situations). The fact that this man dialogs only with himself may indicate that he has cut himself off from others. He is alone with his wealth.

12:18–19 The man's solution for his problem of over-abundance was simply to store up his possessions so he could relax, feast and party.

12:18 tear down ... and build. This is language reminiscent of the prophets, who often spoke of how God would tear down the sinful social structures of Israel and rebuild a pure, holy, social structure in their place (see, for example, Isa. 61:4–7). However, this man will tear down the old only to build larger, new structures that serve the same purpose. Since he is already a rich man prior to this particular harvest, one would assume he already has a large amount of storage capacity. The need (and resources!) to build new buildings accents the miraculous nature of this harvest.

there I will store all my grain and my goods. Up to this point in the story, the listeners would view the man as blessed by God. Even his plan to store the crop for future use could be commended, since the story reverberates with the centuries-old account of how Joseph stored up the abundant crops of Egypt for seven years, so that when the time of famine came he would have resources with which to provide for his people (Gen. 41:33–57). It would be right for this man, blessed by God with this miraculous crop, to store it as God's merciful provision for the people when hard times came upon them. The

32

Leadership Training Supplement

YOU ARE
HERE

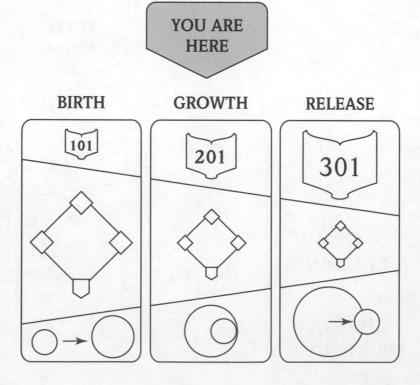

BIRTH	GROWTH	RELEASE
101	201	301

What is the game plan for your group in the 201 stage?

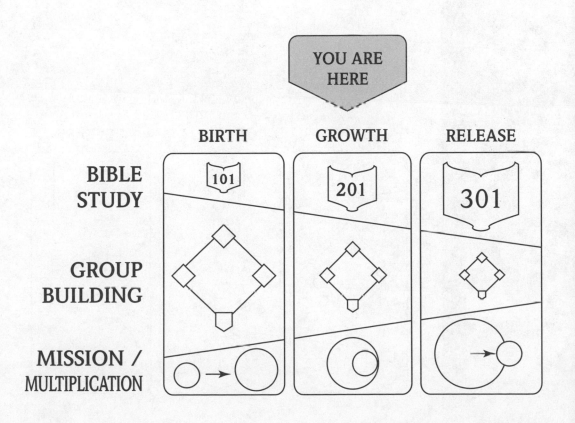

YOU ARE HERE

	BIRTH	GROWTH	RELEASE
BIBLE STUDY	101	201	301
GROUP BUILDING			
MISSION / MULTIPLICATION			

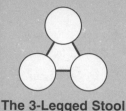

The 3-Legged Stool

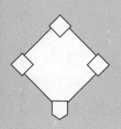

The three essentials in a healthy small group are Bible Study, Group Building and Mission / Multiplication. You need all three to stay balanced—like a 3-legged stool.
- To focus only on Bible Study will lead to scholasticism.
- To focus only on Group Building will lead to narcissism.
- To focus only on Mission will lead to burnout.

You need a game plan for the life cycle of the group where all of these elements are present in a purpose-driven strategy:

Bible Study

To dig into Scripture as a group.

Group Bible Study is quite different from individual Bible Study. The guided discussion questions are open-ended. And for those with little Bible background, there are reference notes to bring this person up to speed.

Group Building

To transform your group into a mission-driven team.

The nine basic needs of a group will be assigned to nine different people. Everyone has a job to fill, and when everyone is doing their job the group will grow spiritually and numerically. When new people enter the group, there is a selection of ICE-BREAKERS to start off the meeting and let the new people get acquainted.

Mission / Multiplication

To identify the Apprentice / Leader for birthing a new group.

In this stage, you will start dreaming about the possibility of starting a new group down the road. The questions at the close of each session will lead you carefully through the dreaming process—to help you discover an Apprentice / Leader who will eventually be the leader of a new group. This is an exciting challenge! (See page M6 for more about Mission / Multiplication.)

Bible Study

What is unique about Serendipity Group Bible Study?

Bible Study for groups is based on six principles. Principle 1: Level the playing field so that everyone can share—those who know the Bible and those who do not know the Bible. Principle 2: Share your spiritual story and let the people in your group get to know you. Principle 3: Ask open-ended questions that have no right or wrong answers. Principle 4: Keep a tight agenda. Principle 5: Subdivide into smaller groups so that everyone can participate. Principle 6: Affirm One Another—"Thanks for sharing."

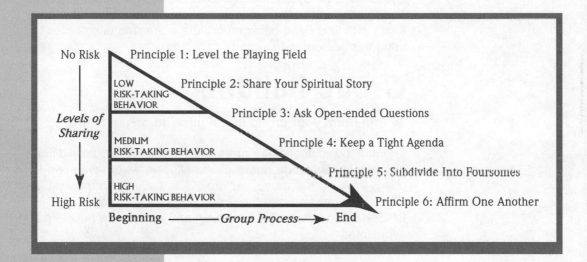

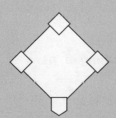

Group Building

What are the jobs that are needed on your team roster?

In the first or second session of this course, you need to fill out the roster on the next page. Then check every few weeks to see that everyone is "playing their position." If you do not have nine people in your group, you can double up on jobs until new people join your group and are assigned a job.

Your Small Group Team Roster

Mission Leader
(Left Field)
Keeps group focused on the mission to invite new people and eventually give birth to a new group. This person needs to be passionate and have a long-term perspective.

_____

Host
(Center Field)
Environmental engineer in charge of meeting location. Always on the lookout for moving to a new meeting location where new people will feel the "home field advantage."

_____

Social Leader
(Right Field)
Designates who is going to bring refreshments. Plans a party every month or so where new people are invited to visit and children are welcome.

_____

Caretaker
(Shortstop)
Takes new members under their wing. Makes sure they get acquainted. Always has an extra book, name tags and a list of group members and phone numbers.

_____

Bible Study Leader
(Second Base)
Takes over in the Bible Study time (30 minutes). Follows the agenda. Keeps the group moving. This person must be very time-conscious.

_____

Group Leader
(Pitcher)
Puts ball in play. Team encourager. Motivator. Sees to it that everyone is involved in the team effort.

_____

Caring Time Leader
(Third Base)
Takes over in the Caring Time. Records prayer requests and follows up on any prayer needs during the week. This person is the "heart" of the group.

_____

Worship Leader
(First Base)
Starts the meeting with singing and prayer. If a new person comes, shifts immediately to an ice-breaker to get acquainted, before the opening prayer.

_____

Apprentice / Leader
(Catcher)
The other half of the battery. Observes the infield. Calls "time" to discuss strategy and regroup. Stays focused.

_____

Mission / Multiplication

Where are you in the 3-stage life cycle of your mission?

You can't sit on a one-legged stool—or even a two-legged stool. It takes all three. The same is true of a small group; you need all three legs. A Bible Study and Care Group will eventually fall if it does not have a mission.

The mission goal is to eventually give birth to a new group. In this 201 course, the goals are: 1) to keep inviting new people to join your group and 2) to discover the Apprentice / Leader and leadership core for starting a new group down the road.

When a new person comes to the group, start off the meeting with one of the ice-breakers on the following pages. These ice-breakers are designed to be fun and easy to share, but they have a very important purpose—that is, to let the new person get acquainted with the group and share their spiritual story with the group, and hear the spiritual stories of those in the group.

YOU ARE HERE

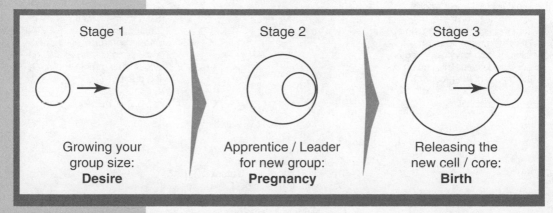

Stage 1	Stage 2	Stage 3
Growing your group size: **Desire**	Apprentice / Leader for new group: **Pregnancy**	Releasing the new cell / core: **Birth**

Ice-Breakers

I Am Somebody Who ...

Rotate around the group, one person reading the first item, the next person reading the second item, etc. Before answering, let everyone in the group try to GUESS what the answer would be: "Yes" ... "No" ... or "Maybe." After everyone has guessed, explain the answer. Anyone who guessed right gets $10. When every item on the list has been read, the person with the most "money" WINS.

I AM SOMEBODY WHO ...

Y N M

☐ ☐ ☐ would go on a blind date
☐ ☐ ☐ sings in the shower
☐ ☐ ☐ listens to music full blast
☐ ☐ ☐ likes to dance
☐ ☐ ☐ cries at movies
☐ ☐ ☐ stops to smell the flowers
☐ ☐ ☐ daydreams a lot
☐ ☐ ☐ likes to play practical jokes
☐ ☐ ☐ makes a "to do" list
☐ ☐ ☐ loves liver
☐ ☐ ☐ won't use a portable toilet
☐ ☐ ☐ likes thunderstorms
☐ ☐ ☐ enjoys romance novels
☐ ☐ ☐ loves crossword puzzles
☐ ☐ ☐ hates flying
☐ ☐ ☐ fixes my own car

Y N M

☐ ☐ ☐ would enjoy skydiving
☐ ☐ ☐ has a black belt in karate
☐ ☐ ☐ watches soap operas
☐ ☐ ☐ is afraid of the dark
☐ ☐ ☐ goes to bed early
☐ ☐ ☐ plays the guitar
☐ ☐ ☐ talks to plants
☐ ☐ ☐ will ask a stranger for directions
☐ ☐ ☐ sleeps until the last second
☐ ☐ ☐ likes to travel alone
☐ ☐ ☐ reads the financial page
☐ ☐ ☐ saves for a rainy day
☐ ☐ ☐ lies about my age
☐ ☐ ☐ yells at the umpire
☐ ☐ ☐ closes my eyes during scary movies

Press Conference

This is a great activity for a new group or when new people are joining an established group. Interview one person with these questions.

1. What is your nickname and how did you get it?

2. Where did you grow up? Where was the "watering hole" in your hometown—where kids got together?

3. What did you do for kicks then? What about now?

4. What was the turning point in your spiritual life?

5. What prompted you to come to this group?

6. What do you want to get out of this group?

Down Memory Lane

Celebrate the childhood memories of the way you were. Choose one or more of the topics listed below and take turns answering the question related to it. If time allows, do another round.

HOME SWEET HOME—What do you remember about your childhood home?

TELEVISION—What was your favorite TV program or radio show?

OLD SCHOOLHOUSE—What were your best and worst subjects in school?

LIBRARY—What did you like to read (and where)?

TELEPHONE—How much time did you spend on the phone each day?

MOVIES—Who was your favorite movie star?

CASH FLOW—What did you do for spending money?

SPORTS—What was your favorite sport or team?

GRANDPA'S HOUSE—Where did your grandparents live? When did you visit them?

POLICE—Did you ever get in trouble with the law?

WEEKENDS—What was the thing to do on Saturday night?

Wallet Scavenger Hunt

With your wallet or purse, use the set of questions below. You get two minutes in silence to go through your possessions and find these items. Then break the silence and "show-and-tell" what you have chosen. For instance, "The thing I have had for the longest time is ... this picture of me when I was a baby."

1. The thing I have had for the LONGEST TIME in my wallet is ...

2. The thing that has SENTIMENTAL VALUE is ...

3. The thing that reminds me of a FUN TIME is ...

4. The most REVEALING thing about me in my wallet is ...

The Grand Total

This is a fun ice-breaker that has additional uses. You can use this ice-breaker to divide your group into two subgroups (odds and evens). You can also calculate who has the highest and lowest totals if you need a fun way to select someone to do a particular task, such as bring refreshments or be first to tell their story.

Fill each box with the correct number and then total your score. When everyone is finished, go around the group and explain how you got your total.

☐ **x**	☐ **=**	☐
Number of hours you sleep	Number of miles you walk daily	Subtotal
☐ **—**	☐ **=**	☐
Number of speeding tickets you've received	Number of times sent to principal's office	Subtotal
☐ **÷**	☐ **=**	☐
Number of hours spent watching TV daily	Number of books you read this year for fun	Subtotal
☐ **+**	☐ **=**	☐
Number of push-ups you can do	Number of pounds you lost this year	Subtotal
		☐
		GRAND TOTAL

Find Yourself in the Picture

In this drawing, which child do you identify with—or which one best portrays you right now? Share with your group which child you would choose and why. You can also use this as an affirmation exercise, by assigning each person in your group to a child in the picture.

Four Facts, One Lie

Everyone in the group should answer the following five questions. One of the five answers should be a lie! The rest of the group members can guess which of your answers is a lie.

1. At age 7, my favorite TV show was ...

2. At age 9, my hero was ...

3. At age 11, I wanted to be a ...

4. At age 13, my favorite music was ...

5. Right now, my favorite pastime is ...

Old-Fashioned Auction

Just like an old-fashioned auction, conduct an out loud auction in your group—starting each item at $50. Everybody starts out with $1,000. Select an auctioneer. This person can also get in on the bidding. Remember, start the bidding on each item at $50. Then, write the winning bid in the left column and the winner's name in the right column. Remember, you only have $1,000 to spend for the whole game. AUCTIONEER: Start off by asking, "Who will give me $50 for a 1965 red MG convertible?" ... and keep going until you have a winner. Keep this auction to 10 minutes.

WINNING BID   WINNER

$_____ 1965 red MG convertible in perfect condition   _____

$_____ Winter vacation in Hawaii for two   _____

$_____ Two Super Bowl tickets on the 50-yard line   _____

$_____ One year of no hassles with my kids / parents   _____

$_____ Holy Land tour hosted by my favorite Christian   _____
                 leader

$_____ Season pass to ski resort of my choice   _____

$_____ Two months off to do anything I want, with pay   _____

$_____ Home theater with surround sound   _____

$_____ Breakfast in bed for one year   _____

$_____ Two front-row tickets at the concert of my choice   _____

$_____ Two-week Caribbean cruise with my spouse in   _____
                 honeymoon suite

$_____ Shopping spree at Saks Fifth Avenue   _____

$_____ Six months of maid service   _____

$_____ All-expense-paid family vacation to Disney World   _____

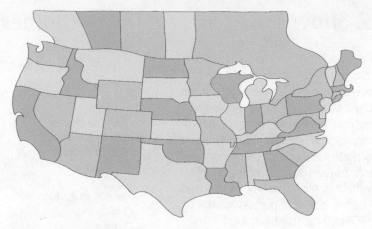

Places in My Life

On the map above, put six dots to indicate these significant places in your journey. Then go around and have each person explain the dots:

- the place where I was born
- the place where I spent most of my life
- the place where I first fell in love
- the place where I went or would like to go on a honeymoon
- the place where God first became real to me
- the place where I would like to retire

The Four Quaker Questions

This is an old Quaker activity which Serendipity has adapted over the years. Go around the group and share your answers to the questions, everyone answering #1. Then, everyone answers #2, etc. This ice-breaker has been known to take between 30 and 60 minutes for some groups.

1. Where were you living between the ages of 7 and 12, and what were the winters like then?

2. How was your home heated during that time?

3. What was the center of warmth in your life when you were a child? (It could be a place in the house, a time of year, a person, etc.)

4. When did God become a "warm" person to you ... and how did it happen?

KWIZ Show

Like a TV quiz show, someone from the group picks a category and reads the four questions—pausing to let the others in the group guess before revealing the answer. When the first person is finished, everyone adds up the money they won by guessing right. Go around the group and have each person take a category. The person with the most money at the end wins. To begin, ask one person to choose a CATEGORY and read out loud the $1 question. Before answering, let everyone try to GUESS the answer. When everyone has guessed, the person answers the question, and anyone who guessed right puts $1 in the margin, etc. until the first person has read all four questions in the CATEGORY.

Clothes

For $1: I'm more likely to shop at:
❏ Sears ❏ Saks Fifth Avenue

For $2: I feel more comfortable wearing:
❏ formal clothes
❏ casual clothes
❏ sport clothes
❏ grubbies

For $3: In buying clothes, I look for:
❏ fashion / style
❏ price
❏ name brand
❏ quality

For $4: In buying clothes, I usually:
❏ shop all day for a bargain
❏ go to one store, but try on everything
❏ buy the first thing I try on
❏ buy without trying it on

Tastes

For $1: In music, I am closer to:
❏ Bach ❏ Beatles

For $2: In furniture, I prefer:
❏ Early American
❏ French Provincial
❏ Scandinavian—contemporary
❏ Hodgepodge—little of everything

For $3: My favorite choice of reading material is:
❏ science fiction ❏ sports
❏ mystery ❏ romance

For $4: If I had $1,000 to splurge, I would buy:
❏ one original painting
❏ two numbered prints
❏ three reproductions and an easy chair
❏ four cheap imitations, an easy chair and a color TV

Travel

For $1: For travel, I prefer:
❏ excitement ❏ enrichment

For $2: On a vacation, my lifestyle is:
❏ go-go all the time
❏ slow and easy
❏ party every night and sleep in

For $3: In packing for a trip, I include:
❏ toothbrush and change of underwear
❏ light bag and good book
❏ small suitcase and nice outfit
❏ all but the kitchen sink

For $4: If I had money to blow, I would choose:
❏ one glorious night in a luxury hotel
❏ a weekend in a nice hotel
❏ a full week in a cheap motel
❏ two weeks camping in the boondocks

Habits

For $1: I am more likely to squeeze the toothpaste:
- ❏ in the middle   ❏ from the end

For $2: If I am lost, I will probably:
- ❏ stop and ask directions
- ❏ check the map
- ❏ find the way by driving around

For $3: I read the newspaper starting with the:
- ❏ front page
- ❏ funnies
- ❏ sports
- ❏ entertainment section

For $4: When I get ready for bed, I put my clothes:
- ❏ on a hanger in the closet
- ❏ folded neatly over a chair
- ❏ into a hamper or clothes basket
- ❏ on the floor

Shows

For $1: I am more likely to:
- ❏ go see a first-run movie
- ❏ rent a video at home

For $2: On TV, my first choice is:
- ❏ news
- ❏ sports
- ❏ sitcoms

For $3: If a show gets too scary, I will usually:
- ❏ go to the restroom
- ❏ close my eyes
- ❏ clutch a friend
- ❏ love it

For $4: In movies, I prefer:
- ❏ romantic comedies
- ❏ serious drama
- ❏ action films
- ❏ Disney animation

Food

For $1: I prefer to eat at a:
- ❏ fast-food restaurant
- ❏ fancy restaurant

For $2: On the menu, I look for something:
- ❏ familiar
- ❏ different
- ❏ way-out

For $3: When eating chicken, my preference is a:
- ❏ drumstick
- ❏ wing
- ❏ breast
- ❏ gizzard

For $4: I draw the line when it comes to eating:
- ❏ frog legs
- ❏ snails
- ❏ raw oysters
- ❏ Rocky Mountain oysters

Work

For $1: I prefer to work at a job that is:
- ❏ too big to handle
- ❏ too small to be challenging

For $2: The job I find most unpleasant to do is:
- ❏ cleaning the house
- ❏ working in the yard
- ❏ balancing the checkbook

For $3: In choosing a job, I look for:
- ❏ salary
- ❏ security
- ❏ fulfillment
- ❏ working conditions

For $4: If I had to choose between these jobs, I would choose:
- ❏ pickle inspector at processing plant
- ❏ complaint officer at department store
- ❏ bedpan changer at hospital
- ❏ personnel manager in charge of firing

Let Me Tell You About My Day

What was your day like today? Use one of the characters below to help you describe your day to the group. Feel free to elaborate.

GREEK TRAGEDY
It was classic, not a dry eye in the house.

EPISODE OF THREE STOOGES
I was Larry, trapped between Curly and Moe.

SOAP OPERA
I didn't think these things could happen, until it happened to me.

ACTION ADVENTURE
When I rode onto the scene, everybody noticed.

BIBLE EPIC
Cecil B. DeMille couldn't have done it any better.

LATE NIGHT NEWS
It might as well have been broadcast over the airwaves.

BORING LECTURE
The biggest challenge of the day was staying awake.

PROFESSIONAL WRESTLING MATCH
I feel as if Hulk Hogan's been coming after me.

FIREWORKS DISPLAY
It was spectacular.

Music in My Life

Put an *"X"* on the first line below—somewhere between the two extremes—to indicate how you are feeling right now. Share your answers, and then repeat this process down the list. If you feel comfortable, briefly explain your response.

IN MY PERSONAL LIFE, I'M FEELING LIKE ...
Blues in the Night_____ Feeling Groovy

IN MY FAMILY LIFE, I'M FEELING LIKE ...
Stormy Weather _____ The Sound of Music

IN MY EMOTIONAL LIFE, I'M FEELING LIKE ...
The Feeling Is Gone _____ On Eagle's Wings

IN MY WORK, SCHOOL OR CAREER, I'M FEELING LIKE ...
Take This Job and Shove It _____ The Future's So Bright I Gotta Wear Shades

IN MY SPIRITUAL LIFE, I'M FEELING LIKE ...
Sounds of Silence _____ Hallelujah Chorus

My Childhood Table

Try to recall the table where you ate most of your meals as a child, and the people who sat around that table. Use the questions below to describe these significant relationships, and how they helped to shape the person you are today.

1. What was the shape of the table?
2. Where did you sit?
3. Who else was at the table?
4. If you had to describe each person with a color, what would be the color of (for instance):
   ❏ Your father? (e.g., dark blue, because he was conservative like IBM)
   ❏ Your mother? (e.g., light green, because she reminded me of springtime)
5. If you had to describe the atmosphere at the table with a color, what would you choose? (e.g., bright orange, because it was warm and light)
6. Who was the person at the table who praised you and made you feel special?
7. Who provided the spiritual leadership in your home?

Home Improvement

Take inventory of your own life. Bob Munger, in his booklet *My Heart—Christ's Home*, describes the areas of a person's life as the rooms of a house. Give yourself a grade on each room as follows, then share with the others your best and worst grade.

❑ A = excellent   ❑ C = passing, needs a little dusting

❑ B = good   ❑ D = passing, but needs a lot of improvement

LIBRARY: This room is in your mind—what you allow to go into it and come out of it. It is the "control room" of the entire house.

DINING ROOM: Appetites, desires; those things your mind and spirit feed on for nourishment.

DRAWING ROOM: This is where you draw close to God—seeking time with him daily, not just in times of distress or need.

WORKSHOP: This room is where your gifts, talents and skills are put to work for God—by the power of the Spirit.

RUMPUS ROOM: The social area of your life; the things you do to amuse yourself and others.

HALL CLOSET: The one secret place that no one knows about, but is a real stumbling block in your walk in the Spirit.

How Is It With Your Soul?

John Wesley, the founder of the Methodist Church, asked his "class meetings" to check in each week at their small group meeting with this question: "How is it with your soul?" To answer this question, choose one of these four allegories to explain the past week in your life:

WEATHER: For example: "This week has been mostly cloudy, with some thunderstorms at midweek. Right now, the weather is a little brighter ..."

MUSIC: For example: "This past week has been like heavy rock music—almost too loud. The sound seems to reverberate off the walls."

COLOR: For example: "This past week has been mostly fall colors—deep orange, flaming red and pumpkin."

SEASON OF THE YEAR: For example: "This past week has been like springtime. New signs of life are beginning to appear on the barren trees, and a few shoots of winter wheat are breaking through the frozen ground."

My Spiritual Journey

The half-finished sentences below are designed to help you share your spiritual story. Ask one person to finish all the sentences. Then move to the next person, etc. If you are short on time, have only one person tell their story in this session.

1. RELIGIOUS BACKGROUND: My spiritual story begins in my home as a child, where the religious training was ...

2. CHURCH: The church that I went to as a child was ...

3. SIGNIFICANT PERSON: The person who had the greatest influence on my spiritual formation was ...

4. PERSONAL ENCOUNTER: The first time God became more than just a name to me was when ...

5. JOURNEY: Since my personal encounter with God, my Christian life might be described as ...

6. PRESENT: On a scale from 1 to 10, I would describe my spiritual energy level right now as a ...

7. NEXT STEP: The thing I need to work on right now in my spiritual life is ...

Bragging Rights

Check your group for bragging rights in these categories.

❏ SPEEDING TICKETS: the person with the most speeding tickets
❏ BROKEN BONES: the person with the most broken bones
❏ STITCHES: the person with the most stitches
❏ SCARS: the person with the longest scar
❏ FISH OR GAME: the person who claims they caught the largest fish or killed the largest animal
❏ STUNTS: the person with the most death-defying story
❏ IRON: the person who can pump the most iron

Personal Habits

Have everyone in your group finish the sentence on the first category by putting an "*X*" somewhere between the two extremes (e.g., on HOUSEWORK ... I would put myself closer to "Where's the floor?"). Repeat this process down the list as time permits.

ON HOUSEWORK, I AM SOMEWHERE BETWEEN:
Eat off the floor_____Where's the floor?

ON COOKING, I AM SOMEWHERE BETWEEN:
Every meal is an act of worship_____Make it fast and hold the frills

ON EXERCISING, I AM SOMEWHERE BETWEEN:
Workout every morning_____Click the remote

ON SHOPPING, I AM SOMEWHERE BETWEEN:
Shop all day for a bargain_____Only the best

ON EATING, I AM SOMEWHERE BETWEEN:
You are what you eat_____Eat, drink and be merry

American Graffiti

If Hollywood made a movie about your life on the night of your high school prom, what would be needed? Let each person in your group have a few minutes to recall these details. If you have more than four or five in your group, ask everyone to choose two or three topics to talk about.

1. LOCATION: Where were you living?
2. WEIGHT: How much did you weigh—soaking wet?
3. PROM: Where was it held?
4. DATE: Who did you go with?
5. CAR / TRANSPORTATION: How did you get there?
    (If you used a car, what was the model, year, color, condition?)
6. ATTIRE: What did you wear?
7. PROGRAM: What was the entertainment?
8. AFTERWARD: What did you do afterward?
9. HIGHLIGHT: What was the highlight of the evening?
10. HOMECOMING: If you could go back and visit your high school, who would you like to see?

Group Orchestra

Read out loud the first item and let everyone nominate the person in your group for this musical instrument in your group orchestra. Then, read aloud the next instrument, and call out another name, etc.

ANGELIC HARP: Soft, gentle, melodious, wooing with heavenly sounds.

OLD-FASHIONED WASHBOARD: Nonconforming, childlike and fun.

PLAYER PIANO: Mischievous, raucous, honky-tonk—delightfully carefree.

KETTLEDRUM: Strong, vibrant, commanding when needed but usually in the background.

PASSIONATE CASTANET: Full of Spanish fervor—intense and always upbeat.

STRADIVARIUS VIOLIN: Priceless, exquisite, soul-piercing—with the touch of the master.

FLUTTERING FLUTE: Tender, lighthearted, wide-ranging and clear as crystal.

SCOTTISH BAGPIPES: Forthright, distinctive and unmistakable.

SQUARE DANCE FIDDLE: Folksy, down-to-earth, toe-tapping—sprightly and full of energy.

ENCHANTING OBOE: Haunting, charming, disarming—even the cobra is harmless with this sound.

MELLOW CELLO: Deep, sonorous, compassionate—adding body and depth to the orchestra.

PIPE ORGAN: Grand, magnificent, rich—versatile and commanding.

HERALDING TRUMPET: Stirring, lively, invigorating—signaling attention and attack.

CLASSICAL GUITAR: Contemplative, profound, thoughtful *and* thought-provoking.

ONE-MAN BAND: Able to do many things well, all at once.

COMB AND TISSUE PAPER: Makeshift, original, uncomplicated—homespun and creative.

SWINGING TROMBONE: Warm, rich—great in solo or background support.

Broadway Show

Imagine for a moment that your group has been chosen to produce a Broadway show, and you have to choose people from your group for all of the jobs for this production. Have someone read out loud the job description for the first job below—PRODUCER. Then, let everyone in your group call out the name of the person in your group who would best fit this job. (You don't have to agree.) Then read the job description for the next job and let everyone nominate another person, etc. You only have 10 minutes for this assignment, so move fast.

PRODUCER: Typical Hollywood business tycoon; extravagant, big-budget, big-production magnate in the Steven Spielberg style.

DIRECTOR: Creative, imaginative brains who coordinates the production and draws the best out of others.

HEROINE: Beautiful, captivating, everybody's heart throb; defenseless when men are around, but nobody's fool.

HERO: Tough, macho, champion of the underdog, knight in shining armor; defender of truth.

COMEDIAN: Childlike, happy-go-lucky, outrageously funny, keeps everyone laughing.

CHARACTER PERSON: Rugged individualist, outrageously different, colorful, adds spice to any surrounding.

FALL GUY: Easy going, nonchalant character who wins the hearts of everyone by being the "foil" of the heavy characters.

TECHNICAL DIRECTOR: The genius for "sound and lights"; creates the perfect atmosphere.

COMPOSER OF LYRICS: Communicates in music what everybody understands; heavy into feelings, moods, outbursts of energy.

PUBLICITY AGENT: Advertising and public relations expert; knows all the angles, good at one-liners, a flair for "hot" news.

VILLAIN: The "bad guy" who really is the heavy for the plot, forces others to think, challenges traditional values; out to destroy anything artificial or hypocritical.

AUTHOR: Shy, aloof; very much in touch with feelings, sensitive to people, puts into words what others only feel.

STAGEHAND: Supportive, behind-the-scenes person who makes things run smoothly; patient and tolerant.

Wild Predictions

Try to match the people in your group to the crazy forecasts below. (Don't take it too seriously; it's meant to be fun!) Read out loud the first item and ask everyone to call out the name of the person who is most likely to accomplish this feat. Then, read the next item and ask everyone to make a new prediction, etc.

THE PERSON IN OUR GROUP MOST LIKELY TO ...

Make a million selling Beanie Babies over the Internet

Become famous for designing new attire for sumo wrestlers

Replace Vanna White on *Wheel of Fortune*

Appear on *The Tonight Show* to exhibit an acrobatic talent

Move to a desert island

Discover a new use for underarm deodorant

Succeed David Letterman as host of *The Late Show*

Substitute for John Madden as Fox's football color analyst

Appear on the cover of *Muscle & Fitness Magazine*

Become the newest member of the Spice Girls

Work as a bodyguard for Rush Limbaugh at Feminist convention

Write a best-selling novel based on their love life

Be a dance instructor on a cruise ship for wealthy, well-endowed widows

Win the blue ribbon at the state fair for best Rocky Mountain oyster recipe

Land a job as head librarian for Amazon.com

Be the first woman to win the Indianapolis 500

Open the Clouseau Private Detective Agency

Career Placements

Read the list of career choices aloud and quickly choose someone in your group for each job—based upon their unique gifts and talents. Have fun!

SPACE ENVIRONMENTAL ENGINEER: in charge of designing the bathrooms on space shuttles

SCHOOL BUS DRIVER: for junior high kids in New York City (earplugs supplied)

WRITER: of an "advice to the lovelorn" column in Hollywood

SUPERVISOR: of a complaint department for a large automobile dealership and service department

ANIMAL PSYCHIATRIST: for French poodles in a fashionable suburb of Paris

RESEARCH SCIENTIST: studying the fertilization patterns of the dodo bird—now extinct

SAFARI GUIDE: in the heart of Africa—for wealthy widows and eccentric bachelors

LITTLE LEAGUE BASEBALL COACH: in Mudville, Illinois—last year's record was 0 and 12

MANAGER: of your local McDonald's during the holiday rush with 210 teenage employees

LIBRARIAN: for the Walt Disney Hall of Fame memorabilia

CHOREOGRAPHER: for the Dallas Cowboys cheerleaders

NURSE'S AIDE: at a home for retired Sumo wrestlers

SECURITY GUARD: crowd control officer at a rock concert

ORGANIZER: of paperwork for Congress

PUBLIC RELATIONS MANAGER: for Dennis Rodman

BODYGUARD: for Rush Limbaugh on a speaking tour of feminist groups

TOY ASSEMBLY PERSON: for a toy store over the holidays

You and Me, Partner

Think of the people in your group as you read over the list of activities below. If you had to choose someone from your group to be your partner, who would you choose to do these activities with? Jot down each person's name beside the activity. You can use each person's name only once and you have to use everyone's name once—so think it through before you jot down their names. Then, let one person listen to what others chose for them. Then, move to the next person, etc., around your group.

WHO WOULD YOU CHOOSE FOR THE FOLLOWING?

_____ ENDURANCE DANCE CONTEST partner

_____ BOBSLED RACE partner for the Olympics

_____ TRAPEZE ACT partner

_____ MY UNDERSTUDY for my debut in a Broadway musical

_____ BEST MAN or MAID OF HONOR at my wedding

_____ SECRET UNDERCOVER AGENT copartner

_____ BODYGUARD for me when I strike it rich

_____ MOUNTAIN CLIMBING partner in climbing Mt. Everest

_____ ASTRONAUT to fly the space shuttle while I walk in space

_____ SAND CASTLE TOURNAMENT building partner

_____ PIT CREW foreman for entry in Indianapolis 500

_____ AUTHOR for my biography

_____ SURGEON to operate on me for a life-threatening cancer

_____ NEW BUSINESS START-UP partner

_____ TAG-TEAM partner for a professional wrestling match

_____ HEAVY-DUTY PRAYER partner

My Gourmet Group

Here's a chance to pass out some much deserved praise for the people who have made your group something special. Ask one person to sit in silence while the others explain the delicacy they would choose to describe the contribution this person has made to your group. Repeat the process for each member of the group.

CAVIAR: That special touch of class and aristocratic taste that has made the rest of us feel like royalty.

PRIME RIB: Stable, brawny, macho, the generous mainstay of any menu; juicy, mouth-watering "perfect cut" for good nourishment.

IMPORTED CHEESE: Distinctive, tangy, mellow with age; adds depth to any meal.

VINEGAR AND OIL: Tart, witty, dry; a rare combination of healing ointment and pungent spice to add "bite" to the salad.

ARTICHOKE HEARTS: Tender and disarmingly vulnerable; whets the appetite for heartfelt sharing.

FRENCH PASTRY: Tempting, irresistible "creme de la creme" dessert; the connoisseur's delight for topping off a meal.

PHEASANT UNDER GLASS: Wild, totally unique, a rare dish for people who appreciate original fare.

CARAFE OF WINE: Sparkling, effervescent, exuberant and joyful; outrageously free and liberating to the rest of us.

ESCARGOT AND OYSTERS: Priceless treasures of the sea once out of their shells; succulent, delicate and irreplaceable.

FRESH FRUIT: Vine-ripened, energy-filled, invigorating; the perfect treat after a heavy meal.

ITALIAN ICE CREAMS: Colorful, flavorful, delightfully childlike; the unexpected surprise in our group.

Thank You

How would you describe your experience with this group? Choose one of the animals below that best describes how your experience in this group affected your life. Then share your responses with the group.

WILD EAGLE: You have helped to heal my wings, and taught me how to soar again.

TOWERING GIRAFFE: You have helped me to hold my head up and stick my neck out, and reach over the fences I have built.

PLAYFUL PORPOISE: You have helped me to find a new freedom and a whole new world to play in.

COLORFUL PEACOCK: You have told me that I'm beautiful; I've started to believe it, and it's changing my life.

SAFARI ELEPHANT: I have enjoyed this new adventure, and I'm not going to forget it, or this group; I can hardly wait for the next safari.

LOVABLE HIPPOPOTAMUS: You have let me surface and bask in the warm sunshine of God's love.

LANKY LEOPARD: You have helped me to look closely at myself and see some spots, and you still accept me the way I am.

DANCING BEAR: You have taught me to dance in the midst of pain, and you have helped me to reach out and hug again.

ALL-WEATHER DUCK: You have helped me to celebrate life—even in stormy weather—and to sing in the rain.

Academy Awards

You have had a chance to observe the gifts and talents of the members of your group. Now you will have a chance to pass out some much deserved praise for the contribution that each member of the group has made to your life. Read out loud the first award. Then let everyone nominate the person they feel is the most deserving for that award. Then read the next award, etc., through the list. Have fun!

SPARK PLUG AWARD: for the person who ignited the group

DEAR ABBY AWARD: for the person who cared enough to listen

ROYAL GIRDLE AWARD: for the person who supported us

WINNIE THE POOH AWARD: for the warm, caring person when someone needed a hug

ROCK OF GIBRALTER AWARD: for the person who was strong in the tough times of our group

OPRAH AWARD: for the person who asked the fun questions that got us to talk

TED KOPPEL AWARD: for the person who asked the heavy questions that made us think

KING ARTHUR'S AWARD: for the knight in shining armor

PINK PANTHER AWARD: for the detective who made us deal with Scripture

NOBEL PEACE PRIZE: for the person who harmonized our differences of opinion without diminishing anyone

BIG MAC AWARD: for the person who showed the biggest hunger for spiritual things

SERENDIPITY CROWN: for the person who grew the most spiritually during the course—in your estimation

You Remind Me of Jesus

Every Christian reflects the character of Jesus in some way. As your group has gotten to know each other, you can begin to see how each person demonstrates Christ in their very own personality. Go around the circle and have each person listen while others take turns telling that person what they notice in him or her that reminds them of Jesus. You may also want to tell them why you selected what you did.

YOU REMIND ME OF ...

JESUS THE HEALER: You seem to be able to touch someone's life with your compassion and help make them whole.

JESUS THE SERVANT: There's nothing that you wouldn't do for someone.

JESUS THE PREACHER: You share your faith in a way that challenges and inspires people.

JESUS THE LEADER: As Jesus had a plan for the disciples, you are able to lead others in a way that honors God.

JESUS THE REBEL: By doing the unexpected, you remind me of Jesus' way of revealing God in unique, surprising ways.

JESUS THE RECONCILER: Like Jesus, you have the ability to be a peacemaker between others.

JESUS THE TEACHER: You have a gift for bringing light and understanding to God's Word.

JESUS THE CRITIC: You have the courage to say what needs to be said, even if it isn't always popular.

JESUS THE SACRIFICE: Like Jesus, you seem willing to sacrifice anything to glorify God.

Reflections

Take some time to evaluate the life of your group by using the statements below. Read the first sentence out loud and ask everyone to explain where they would put a dot between the two extremes. When you are finished, go back and give your group an overall grade in the category of Group Building, Bible Study and Mission.

GROUP BUILDING

On celebrating life and having fun together, we were more like a ...
wet blanket _____ hot tub

On becoming a caring community, we were more like a ...
prickly porcupine_____cuddly teddy bear

BIBLE STUDY

On sharing our spiritual stories, we were more like a ...
shallow pond _____spring-fed lake

On digging into Scripture, we were more like a ...
slow-moving snail _____voracious anteater

MISSION

On inviting new people into our group, we were more like a ...
barbed-wire fence _____wide-open door

On stretching our vision for mission, we were more like an ...
ostrich _____eagle

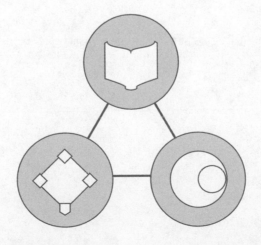

Human Bingo / Party Mixer

After the leader says "Go!" circulate the room, asking people the things described in the boxes. If someone answers "Yes" to a question, have them sign their initials in that box. Continue until someone completes the entire card—or one row if you don't have that much time. You can only use someone's name twice, and you cannot use your own name on your card.

can juggle	TP'd a house	never used an outhouse	sings in the shower	rec'd 6+ traffic tickets	paddled in school	watches Sesame Street
sleeps in church regularly	never changed a diaper	split pants in public	milked a cow	born out of the country	has been to Hawaii	can do the splits
watches soap operas	can touch tongue to nose	rode a motor-cycle	never ridden a horse	moved twice last year	sleeps on a waterbed	has hole in sock
walked in wrong restroom	loves classical music	skipped school	**FREE**	broke a leg	has a hot tub	loves eating sushi
is an only child	loves raw oysters	has a 3-inch + scar	doesn't wear PJ's	smoked a cigar	can dance the Charleston	weighs under 110 lbs.
likes writing poetry	still has tonsils	loves crossword puzzles	likes bubble baths	wearing Fruit of the Loom	doesn't use mouth-wash	often watches cartoons
kissed on first date	can wiggle ears	can play the guitar	plays chess regularly	reads the comics first	can touch palms to floor	sleeps with stuffed animal

Group Covenant

Any group can benefit from creating a group covenant. Reserve some time during one of the first meetings to discuss answers to the following questions. When everyone in the group has the same expectations for the group, everything runs more smoothly.

1.   The purpose of our group is:

2.   The goals of our group are:

3.   We will meet for _____ weeks, after which we will decide if we wish to continue as a group. If we do decide to continue, we will reconsider this covenant.

4.   We will meet _____ (weekly, every other week, monthly).

5.   Our meetings will be from _____ o'clock to _____ o'clock, and we will strive to start and end on time.

6.   We will meet at _____
     or rotate from house to house.

7.   We will take care of the following details: ❏ child care   ❏ refreshments

8.   We agree to the following rules for our group:

     ❏   PRIORITY: While we are in this group, group meetings have priority.

     ❏   PARTICIPATION: Everyone is given the right to their own opinion and all questions are respected.

     ❏   CONFIDENTIALITY: Anything said in the meeting is not to be repeated outside the meeting.

     ❏   EMPTY CHAIR: The group stays open to new people and invites prospective members to visit the group.

     ❏   SUPPORT: Permission is given to call each other in times of need.

     ❏   ADVICE GIVING: Unsolicited advice is not allowed.

     ❏   MISSION: We will do all that is in our power to start a new group.

problem, already hinted at in this verse, is that the man sees it as "my grain and my goods."

12:19 *eat, drink and be merry.* This was a stock phrase from popular caricatures of Epicurean philosophy, which placed the ultimate priority on human pleasure (see also Isa. 22:12–14; 1 Cor. 15:32). Jewish ethics had little respect for this approach to life, since it failed to acknowledge one's responsibility to God and others. It is significant that while the stock phrase ends with "… for tomorrow we die," this man thought that by means of his abundant possessions he might be able to enjoy a life of self-indulgent pleasure for years to come. At this point in the story, the listeners would realize things were going terribly wrong. The man was not following the ways of God, but living as a pagan, concerned only with his own desires. Jewish ethics would echo what Paul makes clear in his letters regarding the purpose of work: first, one is to provide for one's own needs and that of one's family (2 Thess. 3:7–12), and, secondly, one is to give to those in need (Eph. 4:28). The Book of Sirach (a noncanonical but influential Jewish writing) comments, "Blessed is the rich man who is found blameless, and who does not go after gold. Who is he? We call him blessed for he has done wonderful things among his people" (Scott). This man had ample provision for his own needs. Therefore, he should have found storage for the surplus in "the bosoms of the needy, the houses of widows, the mouths of orphans and of infants" (Trench). Instead, he hoards the riches for himself. Failing to see his bumper crop as a gift from God to be shared with others, he sees it as his own possession to be used as he pleases. Ultimately, he also fails to see his life as a gift from God to whom he is responsible for how he lives (v. 20).

12:20 While the man has been the sole character in the story so far, the final word in the parable belongs to God. The ultimate reality of God's judgment shows that making a priority out of seeking wealth for one's own pleasure is meaningless.

You fool! In the Bible, a fool is someone who lives without regard to God.

your life will be demanded from you. The word for "demanded" is a word used in banking circles when a loan was being called in for payment. The man's life, like all his possessions, was a loan from God to whom he is now accountable for its use.

who will get what you have prepared for yourself? This might be understood in two ways: (1) It points out the foolishness of living for material possessions, since at one's death they are of no use to the one who clung to them. He will not be the one to possess what he spent his life preparing to have! (2) It might have been intended to point out his isolation. Having chosen wealth as his god, he is alienated from friends or family. There is no one close to him to whom he can pass on an inheritance when he dies. Greed isolates people from true human relationships.

12:21 *This is how it will be.* Jesus applies the parable to his listeners. Those who are preoccupied with hoarding material provisions for themselves forfeit life with God and alienate themselves from their own families.

rich toward God. Literally, this is "gathering riches for God." Luke 12:33 reveals that one does this by making a priority of giving generously and lavishly to those in need. Disciples can freely give to others because they recognize that God is the provider of all they have and need. Therefore, they need not grasp onto possessions and wealth as though they were in limited supply.

7 Great Banquet—Luke 14:15–24

THREE-PART AGENDA

ICE-BREAKER
15 Minutes

BIBLE STUDY
30 Minutes

CARING TIME
15–45 Minutes

> *LEADER: Check page M7 in the center section for a good ice-breaker, particularly if you have a new person at this meeting. In the Caring Time, is everyone sharing and are prayer requests being followed up?*

TO BEGIN THE BIBLE STUDY TIME
(Choose 1 or 2)

1. When it comes to parties, do you usually arrive: Early? Right on time? "Fashionably late"? Just plain late?

2. Growing up, what was one of your best birthday parties? What made it so great?

3. What social occasion turned out differently than you expected: Your high school prom? Wedding reception? Class reunion? Other?

READ SCRIPTURE & DISCUSS
(If you don't have time for all the questions in this section, conclude the Bible Study [30 min.] by answering question #7.)

1. What is the best excuse you have found for putting something off?

2. What do you think the "great banquet" (v. 16) represents in this parable?

3. What excuses did the invited guests give for not coming to the banquet?

4. How valid were the three excuses given for not attending the banquet (see notes on vv. 18,19 and 20)?

The Parable of the Great Banquet

¹⁵*When one of those at the table with him heard this, he said to Jesus, "Blessed is the man who will eat at the feast in the kingdom of God."*

¹⁶*Jesus replied: "A certain man was preparing a great banquet and invited many guests.* ¹⁷*At the time of the banquet he sent his servant to tell those who had been invited, 'Come, for everything is now ready.'*

¹⁸*"But they all alike began to make excuses. The first said, 'I have just bought a field, and I must go and see it. Please excuse me.'*

¹⁹*"Another said, 'I have just bought five yoke of oxen, and I'm on my way to try them out. Please excuse me.'*

²⁰*"Still another said, 'I just got married, so I can't come.'*

²¹*"The servant came back and reported this to his master. Then the owner of the house became angry and ordered his servant, 'Go out quickly into the streets and alleys of the town and bring in the poor, the crippled, the blind and the lame.'*

²²*" 'Sir,' the servant said, 'what you ordered has been done, but there is still room.'*

²³*"Then the master told his servant, 'Go out to the roads and country lanes and make them come in, so that my house will be full.* ²⁴*I tell you, not one of those men who were invited will get a taste of my banquet.' "*

5. How would you feel as one of "the poor, the crippled, the blind and the lame" (v. 21) brought to the great banquet?

6. What character in this parable can you most identify with?

7. On a scale of 1 (not hungry) to 10 (starving), how would you describe your appetite right now for the things of God?

CARING TIME

(Choose 1 or 2 of these questions before closing in prayer. Be sure to pray for the empty chair.)

1. It's not too late to have someone new come to this group. Who can you invite for next week?

2. Congratulations! You are over halfway through this study. What do you look forward to about coming to this group?

3. How can this group pray for you in the coming week?

Summary. Chapter 14 of Luke's Gospel opens with the story of Jesus at a banquet in the home of a Pharisee. In that setting, he tells his listeners that they should not invite to their feasts and parties only those people who are in a position to repay them, but that they should invite people—like the poor and crippled—who could not be expected to do so. The repayment for these types of hosts will come when they experience the resurrection of the righteous (Luke 14:14). The mention of the resurrection leads one of the dinner guests to express the common Jewish sentiment found in verse 15. Jesus uses this common feeling to underscore the reality of God's gracious invitation and to force his listeners to consider how they have actually responded to God's call.

14:15 *Blessed is the man.* The bliss of life with God was often pictured in terms of a feast (see Isa. 25:6; 65:13). The Jews typically assumed that the messianic banquet was reserved for righteous Jews only. To be "blessed" means to be held in God's favor. It was thought that only those Jews (who by virtue of their good works are accounted righteous) would be able to share in the feast of the Messiah.

14:16–17 *invited / sent his servant to tell.* In well-to-do circles, invitations for a formal dinner were issued well in advance, but the specific time to arrive was communicated on the day of the event when everything was ready (Est. 5:8; 6:14). The double invitation was also an indication of the importance of the guest.

14:18–20 All these people had accepted the invitation earlier. Now that the feast is actually prepared, however, they all offer excuses why they cannot come. In light of their previous acceptance (and the amount of work involved in the preparation of the banquet), Jesus' listeners would immediately see these excuses as a horrible social insult to the host. Some commentators think the excuses are modeled on the provisions for exemptions for military service given in Deuteronomy 20:5–7. When Israel faced war, men who had just bought property, or had planted a vineyard not yet harvested, or had recently married were exempt from military duty. These exceptions were practiced even during the Maccabean revolt against Rome in the second century B.C. Like Jesus' warnings elsewhere (Luke 8:14; 9:23–24,57–62; 12:15), the fact that Jesus uses these excuses demonstrates that normal business and family obligations are not valid reasons for neglecting the call of the kingdom of God. However, since the invitation is to a banquet and not a war, it is questionable whether this is the correct understanding of the excuses. It seems more likely that such excuses would have been understood as an obvious attempt to degrade the host's honor. The guests held him in such low esteem that they would not even dignify their refusal to come with believable reasons. This attitude is reflected by the religious leaders, who were too occupied with their traditions and power to respond to the invitation of Jesus to follow him (Luke 13:34).

14:18 *I have just bought a field, and I must go and see it.* Then, as now, people would not buy property first and then look at it later! Besides, since banquets would be in the late afternoon, the man would have had plenty of time during the day to see it.

14:19 *I'm on my way to try them out.* Just as no one today would buy a used car without a test drive, so then a man would not buy a team of oxen unless he had already tried them out.

14:20 *married.* Marriage plans were made far in advance; the man certainly would have known of his marriage plans when he received the original invitation to the banquet. In this context, the net effect of these excuses is that they are all transparently flimsy. They, in fact, reflect a social snub to the host: they are in effect saying that property, oxen and marital duties are more important than their relationship to the host.

I can't come. At least the first two men politely asked to be excused. The third man simply dismisses the host and his invitation as too insignificant to warrant an apology.

14:21 *streets.* This probably refers to the public squares where beggars would gather, hoping for handouts.

the poor, the crippled, the blind and the lame. Matthew 22:2–14 records a similar parable, but does not specify the condition of those receiving the second invitation. The kinds of people mentioned in this list were all social outcasts, unable to work and reduced to begging for survival. It was commonly assumed their suffering showed that they were being punished by God because of some serious sin they once committed. Throughout his Gospel, Luke has been especially concerned to show that

those normally considered not worthy of the kingdom of God are indeed the ones who are included (Luke 1:52–53; 4:18–19; 6:20–22; 7:22). The irony is highlighted when it is remembered that people with such defects were typically thought of as ritually impure, unable to participate in temple worship and ineligible for taking part in the coming final battle (which would usher in the messianic kingdom for Israel). Jesus shatters these ideas. The kingdom is precisely for these types of people. In contrast, those who were always thought to be "pure" will be excluded. Donahue points out how Jesus shifts attention away from the common apocalyptic expectation of the messianic banquet (as a future, climactic event reserved for the ritually and morally pure) to emphasize how disciples ought to relate to their Lord and to others in the here and now. God's kingdom has come now, and the way disciples treat those who are ordinarily thought to be outcasts (even in religious circles) is a mark of how fully the disciples have caught on to the presence of the King in their midst.

14:23 Since the banquet cannot be filled with only the poor from the city, the servant is sent out to the country to bring in others. Matthew's version of the parable lacks this third invitation to those outside the city. Given Luke's concern for the inclusion of Gentiles in the kingdom of God, he may have included this as a way of foreshadowing the extension of the kingdom of God to include Gentiles (Acts 1:8).

make them come in. This phrase has been unfortunately used in the past to justify forced baptisms and other practices that used political, social or physical pressure to get people to become members of the church. Such practices run counter to the whole spirit of Jesus. The persuasion in view here is simply meant to convince these incredulous outcasts that they really are welcomed to the banquet. Middle East etiquette requires people of a low social rank to refuse invitations from those of a higher social status. The understanding is that such invitations are polite gestures but are not meant to be accepted. "After some discussion the servant will finally have to take the startled guest by the arm and gently pull him along. There is no other way to convince him that he is really invited to the great banquet, irrespective of his being a foreigner" (Bailey).

14:24 *not one ... will get a taste.* It was common for the host of a banquet to send portions of food to those unable to attend. This will not be done in this case because the host will see that the poor eat all of it. None will be left to send to the others. The immediate point of the parable is to warn the religiously privileged Jewish leaders (many of whom were at the table with Jesus—14:3). Their refusal to come to the banquet (which Jesus announced) was rooted in arrogance, and thus was an insult to God. Others will come, but those who refuse the invitation will be excluded (Luke 13:22–30). Hendriksen states, "the one central lesson of the parable is: Accept God's gracious invitation. Do it now!"

The Inclusive Community

A mainline church had a beautiful building in the heart of an old New England city. The founders of the church had long since died, and the neighborhood no longer reflected the social status of those who had founded the church long ago. Once surrounded by elegant homes, the church was now in the center of poorly maintained apartments that had been built up over the years.

Church attendance was so low for so long that the denomination considered closing the church, but a retired minister asked to be given a chance to see if the church could have a viable ministry in the midst of its new surroundings. Since he required no additional income besides his retirement pension, he was allowed to do so. He and a handful of others in the church began to visit throughout the neighborhood to find out what life was like for the people there. They had no agenda; they offered no programs; they simply wanted to meet people, listen, learn, and pray for God's direction.

Some of the neighborhood people began to attend the church. One was a prostitute. Another was a man involved in drug dealings in the city. One longtime member of the church, upset over the presence of such people in what was once such a socially proper church, approached the minister and told him, "I do not want to come to church with whores and drug pushers." The minister placed his hand on her shoulder, looked into her eyes, and replied, "You don't have to. You really don't have to. But you do need to realize that from now on these people will always be welcome to come here. I hope you will too."

8 Builder & King—Luke 14:25–35

THREE-PART AGENDA

ICE-BREAKER
15 Minutes

BIBLE STUDY
30 Minutes

CARING TIME
15–45 Minutes

> **LEADER:** Have you started working with your group about your mission—for instance, by having them review pages M3 and M6 in the center section? If you have a new person at the meeting, remember to do an appropriate ice-breaker from the center section.

TO BEGIN THE BIBLE STUDY TIME
(Choose 1 or 2)

1. Growing up, how did you get along with your brothers and sisters?

2. What was your first car and how much did it cost?

3. How good are you at completing something you've started?

READ SCRIPTURE & DISCUSS
(If you don't have time for all the questions in this section, conclude the Bible Study [30 min.] by answering question #7.)

1. What is your top priority in life right now?

2. In verse 26, what does Jesus mean when he uses the word "hate" in reference to one's family and life?

3. When has a family relationship or close friendship been a hindrance to your wholehearted devotion to Christ?

4. What does Jesus mean when he talks about us carrying our cross?

The Cost of Being a Disciple

[25]*Large crowds were traveling with Jesus, and turning to them he said:* [26]*"If anyone comes to me and does not hate his father and mother, his wife and children, his brothers and sisters—yes, even his own life—he cannot be my disciple.* [27]*And anyone who does not carry his cross and follow me cannot be my disciple.*

[28]*"Suppose one of you wants to build a tower. Will he not first sit down and estimate the cost to see if he has enough money to complete it?* [29]*For if he lays the foundation and is not able to finish it, everyone who sees it will ridicule him,* [30]*saying, 'This fellow began to build and was not able to finish.'*

[31]*"Or suppose a king is about to go to war against another king. Will he not first sit down and consider whether he is able with ten thousand men to oppose the one coming against him with twenty thousand?* [32]*If he is not able, he will send a delegation while the other is still a long way off and will ask for terms of peace.* [33]*In the same way, any of you who does not give up everything he has cannot be my disciple.*

[34]*"Salt is good, but if it loses its saltiness, how can it be made salty again?* [35]*It is fit neither for the soil nor for the manure pile; it is thrown out.*

"He who has ears to hear, let him hear."

5. Based on this passage, what price must a person be willing to pay to be a disciple of Christ?

6. What price have you had to pay to follow Christ? How hard or easy has this been?

7. On a scale of 1 (come again) to 10 (I'm all ears), how receptive are you to Christ's call to discipleship?

CARING TIME
(Choose 1 or 2 of these questions before closing in prayer. Be sure to pray for the empty chair.)

1. How was the weather in your spiritual life last week: Sunny and warm? Scattered showers? Cold and snowy? Other? What's the forecast for the coming week?

2. What is your dream for the future mission of this group?

3. In what specific way can the group pray for you this week?

Summary. While the previous scene used the context of a private dinner party to stress the fact that the invitation to God's kingdom is extended to all types of people (Luke 14:1–24), this scene involves a huge crowd flocking after Jesus. In this context, Jesus lays stress on the serious implications involved in becoming one of his disciples. His intent is not to discourage people from following him, but to give them a clearheaded picture of what discipleship really means. Since the crowds expected the Messiah to bring about a golden age of victory for the Jews (which would insure their prosperity and freedom), it was especially important that they realize the true nature of what discipleship involved. Before the kingdom would fully come, Jesus had to face the Cross. The fact that the Messiah would suffer (and that his people would as well) was not a reality they had comprehended.

14:25 *Large crowds were traveling with Jesus.* Jesus is heading toward Jerusalem for Passover (Luke 9:51). This crowd probably consisted of other pilgrims on the way to the feast as well. The expectations would have been high that Jesus, if he was indeed the Messiah, would begin the establishment of his kingdom at this feast (since it was the celebration of Israel's deliverance from Egypt centuries before). Now the crowd would be expecting him to lead them in deliverance from Rome.

14:26 In contrast to the expectant, exuberant nature of the crowds, Jesus introduces a solemn challenge. While the invitation to the kingdom is extended to all, only those who make Jesus their primary loyalty will participate in it. One's loyalty to Jesus and the kingdom must take precedence over all other commitments, including those that people normally take for granted as primary responsibilities.

comes to me. This is to take on the role of a disciple, one committed to the teachings of a master.

hate. Jesus often used dramatic, overstated examples to arrest people's attention and make his point (see Matt. 5:29–30). His use of the word "hate" here is a hyperbolic way of saying that one's love and loyalty to Jesus must exceed what one naturally has toward one's family. The disciple is to view even normal and ordinarily proper concerns, ambitions, and interests as secondary in importance to the kingdom of God. "Jesus calls not for an unloving attitude, but for a willingness to put him first in the concrete situation where the calls of Jesus and of family conflict" (France). This idea is stated more positively in Matthew 10:37–38 which reads, "Anyone who loves his father or mother more than me is not worthy of me; anyone who loves his son or daughter more than me is not worthy of me; and anyone who does not take his cross and follow me is not worthy of me." This does not justify abandonment of one's responsibilities to family for self-interest under the guise of discipleship, but is simply a call for wholehearted commitment, even when that commitment tears at the very heart of our identity and being. "… it is natural for men and women to make what provision they can for their nearest and dearest. Jesus' emphasis lay rather on the necessity of treating the kingdom of God as nearer and dearer still. Because of the natural resistance on the part of his hearers to accepting this necessity with literal seriousness, he insisted on it in the most arresting and challenging language at his command" (Bruce).

even his own life. Even the instinctive drive for self-preservation must give way to obedience to the call of Jesus. While this seems like a harsh demand, Jesus himself practiced it as he gave his life in order to bring life to others.

14:27 *carry his cross.* Discipleship's total commitment is emphasized even more by this idea.

> *"Just as one should not attempt a venture without having sufficient resources to complete it, but will need to put everything into it in order to be successful, so the disciple must be continually ready … to give up all that he has got in order to follow Jesus."*

cross. This symbolized the grisly method of Roman execution. While it had a very literal application for some disciples, it is meant as a metaphor emphasizing the need for all of Jesus' disciples to put to death one's own desires and interests for the sake of loyalty to Jesus. This statement echoes the one in Luke 9:23, where Luke inserts the word "daily,"

indicating that following Jesus is a day-by-day decision in light of the new pressures and conflicts one continually faces.

14:28–33 In this section, Jesus uses three parables to communicate the need for serious consideration of what it means to be his disciple.

14:28–30 The first parable relates to the daily experience of Jesus' audience. The tower in view might be a vineyard tower used as a lookout to watch for thieves, a storage shed, or some other type of farm building. It would be humiliating to have to stop construction because one planned so poorly that money ran out after only the foundation was completed. In the same way, one must consider the implications of following Jesus. To do so is a commitment of one's entire life and resources. Just as it would be foolish to begin building a tower before one contemplated the costs involved, so Jesus is discouraging people from following him based upon wrong assumptions and ideas of what his kingdom involves.

14:31–32 The second parable reinforces the point of the first. Only a foolish king would attempt to wage a war before considering whether there is realistic hope for success. If the enemy has a far superior force, it would be far better to make a peaceful settlement before hostilities begin than to plunge into destruction. Likewise, a would-be disciple had better first consider what is involved in the course he or she is undertaking. Jesus is not interested in having people following him who are misguided by false expectations.

14:33 *any of you who does not give up everything he has.* The point of both parables is here: "… discipleship means saying a final 'good-bye' to one's possessions (and all other loyalties, ambitions, etc.). Just as one should not attempt a venture without having sufficient resources to complete it, but will need to put everything into it in order to be successful, so the disciple must be continually

ready … to give up all that he has got in order to follow Jesus" (Marshall).

14:34 The final parable builds on the point of the earlier two as it looks at the fate of those who make only a partial attempt to follow Jesus and the way of the kingdom.

Salt is good. Good salt was used to preserve and flavor food. It was also used in small amounts as a way of fertilizing soil and manure to be more productive for the bearing of crops (as is reflected in v. 35).

if it loses its saltiness. True salt, of course, never loses its saltiness. However, Jesus is commenting on what was a common observation of the time for people who lived around the Dead Sea. The evaporation of water from the Dead Sea resulted in white crystals. Some of these crystals were true salt, but others, although they physically looked like salt, were gypsum (which was either bitter or stale). Thus, it appeared that some "salt" was good and other "salt" had apparently somehow lost its valuable properties. While people of the time did not know the chemical realities involved, they did know that there was no way such useless "salt" could ever be restored.

14:35 *it is thrown out.* While the useless crystals looked the same as real salt, they had no function other than to serve as road dust. Failure to persevere with Jesus is to be like these crystals which, while they have the appearance of being real, are worthless.

He who has ears to hear, let him hear. This is a common phrase Jesus used in other contexts as well (see Luke 8:8; Mark 4:9,23). Jesus urges his hearers to ponder his parables. Part of the power of a parable lies in the fact that people must reflect on it in order to understand it. The question is: What insight do they need to grasp about their spiritual life from these simple stories?

9 The Tenants—Mark 12:1–12

THREE-PART AGENDA

ICE-BREAKER
15 Minutes

BIBLE STUDY
30 Minutes

CARING TIME
15–45 Minutes

> *LEADER: To help you identify an Apprentice / Leader for a new small group (or if you have a new person at this meeting), see the listing of ice-breakers on page M7 of the center section.*

TO BEGIN THE BIBLE STUDY TIME
(Choose 1 or 2)

1. When have you rented an apartment or house? What was your landlord like?

2. What kind of fort, tree house or hideout did you have as a kid?

3. If you were to start your own business, what might it be?

READ SCRIPTURE & DISCUSS
(If you don't have time for all the questions in this section, conclude the Bible Study [30 min.] by answering question #7.)

1. When is a time you faced rejection?

2. In this parable, who is represented by the landowner? The tenants? The servants? The son?

3. Who are the "others" that the owner of the vineyard will give the vineyard to?

4. Who is "The stone the builders rejected" (v. 10)? What function does a capstone have? What event was Jesus predicting by telling this story?

The Parable of the Tenants

12 *He then began to speak to them in parables: "A man planted a vineyard. He put a wall around it, dug a pit for the winepress and built a watchtower. Then he rented the vineyard to some farmers and went away on a journey. ²At harvest time he sent a servant to the tenants to collect from them some of the fruit of the vineyard. ³But they seized him, beat him and sent him away empty-handed. ⁴Then he sent another servant to them; they struck this man on the head and treated him shamefully. ⁵He sent still another, and that one they killed. He sent many others; some of them they beat, others they killed.*

⁶"He had one left to send, a son, whom he loved. He sent him last of all, saying, 'They will respect my son.'

⁷"But the tenants said to one another, 'This is the heir. Come, let's kill him, and the inheritance will be ours.' ⁸So they took him and killed him, and threw him out of the vineyard.

⁹"What then will the owner of the vineyard do? He will come and kill those tenants and give the vineyard to others. ¹⁰Haven't you read this scripture:

" 'The stone the builders rejected
has become the capstone[a]*;*
¹¹the Lord has done this, and it is
marvelous in our eyes' [b]*?"*

¹²Then they looked for a way to arrest him because they knew he had spoken the parable against them. But they were afraid of the crowd; so they left him and went away.

[a] *10 Or cornerstone*   [b] *11 Psalm 118:22,23*

5. Why did the tenants believe if they killed the owner's son "the inheritance" (v. 7) would be theirs?

6. How do you feel about working in God's vineyard? What inheritance are you looking forward to receiving from God?

7. How have you been relating to God's authority over your life lately?

CARING TIME

(Choose 1 or 2 of these questions before closing in prayer. Be sure to pray for the empty chair.)

1. Have you started to work on your group mission— to choose an Apprentice / Leader from this group to start a new group in the future? (See Mission / Multiplication on p. M3.)

2. If this group is helping to hold you accountable for something, how are you doing in that area? If not, what is something for which you would like this group to hold you accountable?

3. What prayer needs or praises would you like to share?

43

Summary. This parable (also found in Matt. 21:33–46 and Luke 20:9–19) immediately follows the controversy Jesus stirred up by his radical action of throwing out the money changers in the temple (Mark 11:12–19). The religious authorities who challenged his right to do such a thing were silenced by his artful response (which raised the issue of the authority of John the Baptist, the recently executed leader who had an enormous popular following). This question put the religious leaders in the politically impossible position of either denouncing John the Baptist as a false prophet, or explaining why they failed to heed his word (Mark 11:27–33). While this dilemma led them to back off from their confrontation with Jesus, he refused to simply leave them in their confusion. Instead, Jesus kept up the pressure by speaking this parable which, while it was addressed to the crowd at large, was clearly directed at the leaders. Most parables are deliberately vague so as to force the listener to consider what is truly being said, but the point of this parable was startlingly clear. In no uncertain terms, Jesus was asserting that the leaders of Israel (who have turned against both him and John the Baptist) have rejected God's messengers and so face the prospect of divine judgment.

12:1 *parables.* Typically, a parable has a single point. In such parables, details simply add to the setting of the story (as, for example, in the Parable of the Mustard Seed where the "birds of the air" have no symbolic value, but simply accent the size of the plant that grows from the seed—Mark 4:30–32). This parable, however, is more of an allegory (in that a number of details have meaning). The Parable of the Tenants and the Parable of the Weeds (Matt. 13:24–30,36–43) are more allegorical than any of the other parables.

A man planted a vineyard ... dug a pit ... built a watchtower. For the religious leaders, Jesus' use of these phrases would surely call to mind the well-known imagery found in a poem originally delivered by the prophet Isaiah centuries before (Isa. 5:1–7). In Isaiah's song, the symbol of the vineyard was used to describe Israel. Although planted and cultivated by God, Israel was compared to a vineyard that produced only bad fruit. As a result, the landowner destroyed it. With this similarity established in Isaiah's poem, Jesus goes on to make a significant difference: Isaiah identified the unresponsive vineyard as the nation of Israel as a whole, whereas Jesus focuses attention on the fact that Israel's leaders are like evil tenants who refused to acknowledge God's authority over them.

vineyard. Since grapes were one of the major crops in Israel, a vineyard would be something known to everyone. Grapes were eaten fresh, made into raisins, boiled into a syrup, or made into wine.

a wall. The wall would be to keep out animals and thieves.

a pit. The pit was a place in which the grapes were crushed to make wine.

a watchtower. This was a structure in the midst of the vineyard from which the farmer could keep a lookout for robbers. During the harvest, the farmer would even spend the night in the watchtower. The wall, pit, and tower all emphasize that the farmer intended that this vineyard be productive, since he made such an investment of money and labor in it.

went away. Jesus changes the Isaiah poem here in order to put the spotlight on the religious authorities (who were the leaders of Israel). In Isaiah, God is the farmer who waits for the fruit which never appears; in this parable, God is the landlord who leaves his vineyard in the care of others who are responsible to him. It produces fruit, but the tenants refuse to give him his share of the produce. Absentee landlords were common in the first century, especially in Galilee. Such a landlord would get tenant-farmers to work his large estate, requiring them to give him a portion of their harvest in payment for use of the land. The tenant-farmers frequently resented the landlord.

12:2 *servant.* The landowner's servant came in the name of the landowner and should have been given the proceeds due to the landowner. In terms of this parable, the servants represent the Old Testament prophets. In the Old Testament, prophets were frequently referred to in this way (see Jer. 7:25–26; Zech. 1:6). The fate of the servants in this parable (vv. 2–5) was the same for many of God's prophets. Elijah was scorned by King Ahab. Tradition holds that Isaiah was executed by being sawn in two. Jeremiah faced many struggles, including being cast into a cistern to starve, and being taken as a prisoner to Egypt (where, tradition teaches, he was killed). John the Baptist, believed by the crowds

here in this scene to be a prophet, was beheaded by King Herod with no word of protest from the religious leaders.

12:3–5 The tenants refused to acknowledge the landowner's rights and badly abused those he sent as his representatives.

12:6 *a son, whom he loved.* Neither the crowd nor the religious leaders would have known the identity of the son in this story. The context of the controversy (in which the leaders were rejecting the authority of Jesus) would suggest to the leaders that Jesus was referring to himself, yet he does not explicitly say so. This would create another level of controversy among the leaders. Not only would they be upset at Jesus for identifying them as the evil tenants, but they would also be angered over this implicit claim to be the beloved son of God. While the leaders and the crowd may be confused over who the son represents, Mark's readers know that this is clearly a reference to Jesus. A central theme in Mark 11–16 is the discovery that Jesus is the Son of God. Here is the first clear hint of this on the lips of Jesus (though, of course, God has twice declared him to be such, using the very phrase found here—see 1:11; 9:7). The claim to be God's son was a claim to a unique, intimate relationship with God.

They will respect my son. While the servants had been badly abused, the landowner assumed the tenants would not dare treat his own son with such contempt.

12:7 *inheritance.* The arrival of the son was mistakenly understood by the servants as a sign that the landowner must have died. Assuming that the son had come to claim his inheritance, they decided to take decisive action. By law, a piece of ownerless property could be kept by those who first occupied and cultivated it. Since the tenants assumed the land would be ownerless if the son was dead, they plotted to kill him in order to lay claim to the land for themselves.

12:8 *killed him, and threw him out of the vineyard.* Not only did the tenants fail to respect the son, but they even refused to give him a proper burial. This would have been considered a monstrous indignity to the listeners. Mark's readers, of course, would see the parallels with what happened with Jesus who was crucified, and whose body the reli-

gious leaders would have been content to leave hanging on the cross, were it not for the intervention of Joseph of Arimathea (Mark 15:43).

12:9 This final rejection moves the landowner to take action personally. His sudden, unexpected appearance would shatter the illusion that the tenants now owned the land. The owner could enlist the aid of the government to execute judgment upon the tenants.

give the vineyard to others. The landowner would then rent the vineyard to people who would meet the terms of their contract. The implication in the parable is that God will raise up new leaders to care for his people. In the context in which Mark was written (to Christians in Rome), this was probably understood as an explanation as to why the leadership in the church was becoming filled by more and more Gentiles.

12:10 *The stone the builders rejected has become the capstone.* This quote is from Psalm 118:22. In that context, it refers to how God established David as king even when his enemies attempted to defeat him. Rabbis later interpreted this stone to refer to Abraham, David, or the Messiah. Several New Testament authors quote this as reference to Jesus (Acts 4:11; Eph. 2:20; 1 Peter 2:7). The identification here of the Messiah (the stone) with the Son of God (v. 6) was unique to Jesus. The original image refers to a stone that was rejected as a foundation stone in the building of the sanctuary of Solomon's temple (the first temple). Later on, however, it was found to be the capstone to the main porch (a capstone was the key stone which held an arch in place). In the parable, the stone is Jesus (the Messiah) whom the builders (the leaders) fail to recognize.

12:12 The leaders knew exactly which part they played in Jesus' parable. They were being cast in the role of the evil tenants who killed the servants (prophets) and the heir. From their point of view, such teaching had to be stopped. Not only was Jesus attacking them, but he was implying claims about himself (i.e., that he was the Messiah and God's Son) that they could not tolerate. Yet, because of Jesus' popularity with the crowds (for the way he attacked the abuses in the temple system), they could do nothing at this time.

10 The Talents—Matthew 25:14–30

THREE-PART AGENDA

ICE-BREAKER
15 Minutes

BIBLE STUDY
30 Minutes

CARING TIME
15–45 Minutes

> *LEADER: Check page M7 in the center section for a good ice-breaker, particularly if you have a new person at this meeting. Is your group working well together—with everyone "fielding their position" as shown on the team roster on page M5?*

TO BEGIN THE BIBLE STUDY TIME
(Choose 1 or 2)

1. Growing up, were you more of a saver or spender? How about now?

2. What's the best investment you've ever made?

3. What's something others have told you you're good at?

READ SCRIPTURE & DISCUSS
(If you don't have time for all the questions in this section, conclude the Bible Study [30 min.] by answering question #7.)

1. If you were to go away for a long time, who would you entrust to look after things for you?

2. In this parable, what were the master's expectations of his servants while he was away?

3. Why did the servant given one talent hide his money? Why was the master so hard on this servant?

4. What did the master say to the two servants who doubled his money?

The Parable of the Talents

¹⁴*"Again, it will be like a man going on a journey, who called his servants and entrusted his property to them. ¹⁵To one he gave five talents*[a] *of money, to another two talents, and to another one talent, each according to his ability. Then he went on his journey. ¹⁶The man who had received the five talents went at once and put his money to work and gained five more. ¹⁷So also, the one with the two talents gained two more. ¹⁸But the man who had received the one talent went off, dug a hole in the ground and hid his master's money.*

¹⁹*"After a long time the master of those servants returned and settled accounts with them. ²⁰The man who had received the five talents brought the other five. 'Master,' he said, 'you entrusted me with five talents. See, I have gained five more.'*

²¹*"His master replied, 'Well done, good and faithful servant! You have been faithful with a few things; I will put you in charge of many things. Come and share your master's happiness!'*

²²*"The man with the two talents also came. 'Master,' he said, 'you entrusted me with two talents; see, I have gained two more.'*

²³*"His master replied, 'Well done, good and faithful servant! You have been faithful with a few things; I will put you in charge of many things. Come and share your master's happiness!'*

²⁴*"Then the man who had received the one talent came. 'Master,' he said, 'I knew that you are a hard man, harvesting where you have not sown and gathering where you have not scattered seed. ²⁵So I was afraid and went out and hid your talent in the ground. See, here is what belongs to you.'*

²⁶*"His master replied, 'You wicked, lazy servant! So you knew that I harvest where I have not sown and gather where I have not scattered seed? ²⁷Well then, you should have put my money on deposit with the bankers, so that when I returned I would have received it back with interest.*

²⁸*" 'Take the talent from him and give it to the one who has the ten talents. ²⁹For everyone who has will be given more, and he will have an abundance. Whoever does not have, even what he has will be taken from him. ³⁰And throw that worthless servant outside, into the darkness, where there will be weeping and gnashing of teeth.' "*

[a] 15 A talent was worth more than a thousand dollars.

5. How would you feel about being given more responsibility as the reward for a "job well done"?

6. What right does God have to your talents and why? What is one talent you have that you are using or can use in service to God?

7. What would help you to better use your talents and abilities: To recognize them? To be more responsible? To believe in yourself? To get more encouragement from others? To trust in God more?

CARING TIME

(Choose 1 or 2 of these questions before closing in prayer.)

1. How are you doing at spending personal time in prayer and Bible study?

2. How is the group doing "fielding their positions," as shown on the team roster (p. M5)?

3. What would you like to share with the group for prayer this week?

Notes—Matthew 25:14-30

Summary. This parable is a different version of the one in Luke 19:11–27. While sharing a common story, the authors apply it in different ways. The major emphasis of the parable in Luke is to prepare the disciples for the delay in the coming of God's kingdom, and to warn the enemies of Jesus regarding their fate when Christ's kingdom comes. Matthew uses the parable as the third of four stories to: (1) encourage the disciples to continue in active service for the kingdom, even while its appearance is delayed and, (2) warn the disciples not to be negligent of their responsibilities in light of the judgment which, though delayed, is sure to come (24:42–44). By means of the parable, Jesus underscores three points to the disciples: (1) His kingdom as they imagine it will not be established at this time; (2) Discipleship means faithful service to God while awaiting Christ's return, and (3) Judgment awaits those who fail to invest themselves in the work of the kingdom.

25:14 *a man ... called his servants and entrusted his property to them.* Wealthy people who had to travel on business would entrust their resources to capable servants who would act as managers of the estate. Their responsibility was to look after their master's interests in his absence, investing his resources in a way that would earn more money for him.

25:15 *five talents.* A talent was originally a unit of weight, but was also used as the name for the highest denomination of coinage. While exact modern parallels are impossible to make, Henderson notes that in the time of Jesus it would take a laborer almost 20 years to earn the equivalent of one talent!

each according to his ability. The master took into account the level of responsibility he believed each servant could handle. Each would be evaluated only in terms of what had been entrusted to him.

25:16–18 Like today, investing money always carried with it the risk that one might lose it. Yet two of the servants are reported as having had very good returns of their investments. The third servant, however, failed to do anything constructive with the money he was given to manage.

25:16 *gained five more.* High interest rates in that time could make a thousand percent return possible (though undoubtedly difficult).

25:18 *dug a hole in the ground and hid his master's money.* In the absence of safe deposit boxes, this was not an uncommon occurrence as a way of protecting one's money from being stolen. This would have been considered a safe way to protect money, but obviously its investment possibilities are nil!

25:19 *After a long time.* The indefinite time reference is to prepare the disciples for the realization that the final coming of the kingdom is still far off. They should not be surprised at its delay.

settled accounts. This was the time of reckoning, in which the master would evaluate how the various servants had done in fulfilling their responsibility to him.

25:20 *See.* The emphasis here is on the fact that the servant welcomes the master's inspection because he knows he has done a good job.

25:21 *Well done, good and faithful servant!* The servant's faithfulness in this matter is the quality that allows the master to trust him with greater responsibility (see also Luke 12:42–44).

few things / many things. The servant is rewarded, not with a life of ease, but with greater administrative responsibility in the master's household (based on the master's trust and confidence in him). While five talents is by no means something small, the point is that they are "a few things" in comparison with the responsibility he will now be entrusted to handle.

Come and share your master's happiness. The servant is not only given more responsibility, but now is invited to enjoy camaraderie with the master. The relationship has shifted from simply a master/servant arrangement to one of friendship and mutual respect.

25:24–25 In contrast to the other two, this servant had simply hidden the money away where it did no good. The servant's reasoning for doing so was based on his fear of failing to live up to the master's high expectations. He assumed it would be better to safely return the money rather than risk having to make up any loss he may have incurred by making a bad investment.

25:24 *a hard man.* Literally, this is "exacting." The description of the master is uncomplimentary; it pictures him as ruthless, harvesting for himself the fruits for which other people have worked. While the inclinations of the listeners (who were poor) might naturally lead them to favor the servant over a "hard" rich man, nothing in the story so far indicates that the servant's characterization of the master was correct. He was generous in his original entrustment of his property to the servants; he was generous to the first and second servants upon his return. It would raise the question in the listeners' minds as to whether the servant was correct or just irresponsible in light of such a generous master's trust.

25:25 *So I was afraid.* The servant implies that his lack of having anything to show for having been entrusted with the talent is really the fault of the master: He expects too much; he is too frightening.

here is what belongs to you. Rabbinic teaching emphasized that God had given Israel the responsibility to protect the Law until the time came when he would establish his kingdom. Given that this parable occurs just prior to Jesus' death, it may be that Jesus has this tradition in mind with this parable. While the Pharisees have "protected" the Law from being corrupted by the masses, they have failed to use it in a way that would draw others to God. They can only return it to God intact, but without being able to show any benefit from having been entrusted with it. Thus, their judgment is assured. His disciples are to do better than that.

25:26–27 The servant stands condemned by his own words. Whether or not his assessment of the master was correct, if he felt that the master was like this he should have at least tried to make some safe investments so that there would be at least a little bit of profit to show.

25:26 *You wicked, lazy servant.* The master turns the tables on the servant. It was not out of fear of him that the servant acted as he did; it was because he did not have the master's interests at heart. His action did not betray a wise fear of the master's authority, but simply neglect of his responsibility. If the servant was so certain of the master's character, he would have been sure to have done something so that he would not have to face the master with nothing to show for the master's trust in him.

25:27 *on deposit.* Literally, the phrase here is "on the table." The table used by money changers in Jerusalem is in view. The servant could have at least invested the money in this way. All financial dealings in the temple had to be conducted in local currency. For example, at Passover each Jew was required to pay a temple tax of one-half shekel (nearly two days' wages for a laborer). Since no other currency was acceptable, money changers would exchange foreign currency for that used in Jerusalem. However, they charged exorbitant amounts for the simple act of exchanging currency: up to one-half day's wages for a working person. Thus, to invest the money with these money changers guaranteed a high rate of return. The parable is not meant to condone this practice; indeed, it was this exploitative rate of interest that led Jesus to forcibly protest this practice in the temple (Matt. 21:12–13). The story simply uses this practice as a fact of life the hearers would have understood.

25:28–30 Judgment is pronounced upon this servant. The faithless servant loses the capital he had been given, while it is added to the interest of the most faithful servant. By doing so, the master shows that the faithless servant's characterization of him as hard and miserly is false. The point of this part of the parable is to warn the disciples to apply themselves to the task of serving Jesus with all diligence. "There is no such thing as standing still in the Christian life" (Barclay). God expects those to whom he has entrusted various gifts to be faithful and diligent in their use of them for his purposes.

25:29 *For everyone who has ...* The judgment is justified by use of a common saying found in other contexts as well (Matt. 13:12; Mark 4:25; Luke 8:18). The saying illustrates a spiritual principle about discipleship that has many implications. In brief, those who hear and practice the word from God that they have been given are those who will be able to understand and receive more from God. Those who neglect what they have already heard will not be given any more.

25:30 *throw that worthless servant outside, into the darkness, where there will be weeping and gnashing of teeth.* This is a graphic, stock phrase often used to express the severity of God's judgment (see Matt. 8:12; 13:42,50; 22:13; 24:5; Luke 13:28).

11 Workers in Vineyard—Matt. 20:1–16

THREE-PART AGENDA

ICE-BREAKER
15 Minutes

BIBLE STUDY
30 Minutes

CARING TIME
15–45 Minutes

> *LEADER: To help you identify an Apprentice / Leader and the people who might form the core of a new small group, see the listing of ice-breakers on page M7 of the center section.*

TO BEGIN THE BIBLE STUDY TIME
(Choose 1 or 2)

1. When you were a child, what chores were you expected to do? What kind of allowance did you receive?

2. What's the best job you've ever had? The worst?

3. When have you received something you weren't expecting or didn't deserve?

READ SCRIPTURE & DISCUSS
(If you don't have time for all the questions in this section, conclude the Bible Study [30 min.] by answering question #7.)

1. In looking for work, which is more important to you—the pay or the personal fulfillment the job offers?

2. If you had been one of the first workers hired, how would you have felt at pay time?

3. How do you think the VWU (Vineyard Worker's Union) would look upon the owner's compensation plan?

4. Is the landowner's business practice unjust or generous?

The Parable of the Workers in the Vineyard

20 *"For the kingdom of heaven is like a landowner who went out early in the morning to hire men to work in his vineyard. ²He agreed to pay them a denarius for the day and sent them into his vineyard.*

³"About the third hour he went out and saw others standing in the marketplace doing nothing. ⁴He told them, 'You also go and work in my vineyard, and I will pay you whatever is right.' ⁵So they went.

"He went out again about the sixth hour and the ninth hour and did the same thing. ⁶About the eleventh hour he went out and found still others standing around. He asked them, 'Why have you been standing here all day long doing nothing?'

⁷" 'Because no one has hired us,' they answered.

"He said to them, 'You also go and work in my vineyard.'

⁸"When evening came, the owner of the vineyard said to his foreman, 'Call the workers and pay them their wages, beginning with the last ones hired and going on to the first.'

⁹"The workers who were hired about the eleventh hour came and each received a denarius. ¹⁰So when those came who were hired first, they expected to receive more. But each one of them also received a denarius. ¹¹When they received it, they began to grumble against the landowner. ¹²'These men who were hired last worked only one hour,' they said, 'and you have made them equal to us who have borne the burden of the work and the heat of the day.'

¹³"But he answered one of them, 'Friend, I am not being unfair to you. Didn't you agree to work for a denarius? ¹⁴Take your pay and go. I want to give the man who was hired last the same as I gave you. ¹⁵Don't I have the right to do what I want with my own money? Or are you envious because I am generous?'

¹⁶"So the last will be first, and the first will be last."

5. What have you found the working conditions to be like in God's vineyard?

6. How would you describe your attitude toward your job right now? Toward God's work?

7. What does this parable say to you about God and his kingdom?

CARING TIME
(Choose 1 or 2 of these questions before closing in prayer.)

1. Who would you choose as the leader if this group "gave birth" to a new small group? Who else would you choose to be a part of the leadership core for a new group?

2. How has God been at work in your life this past week?

3. What prayer requests do you have for this week?

Summary. This parable follows Jesus' response to the disciples' concern about who will be able to enter God's kingdom (Matt. 19:25). Jesus assured them that those who follow him will receive far more than they ever gave up in order to become disciples. He then adds, "But many who are first will be last, and many who are last will be first" (Matt. 19:30), a phrase echoed at the end of this parable (v. 16—see also Luke 13:30). The point of the saying is to relieve the disciples of any notion that the length of time a person knows Jesus has any bearing on one's ultimate relationship with him. The nature of one's relationship with Jesus is a matter of God's grace, not a matter of how one has ranked in time or how much religious merit one has tried to accumulate. This would have been an issue for the church in Matthew's day in a couple of ways: (1) They may have wondered if their discipleship was somehow second-rate (since they had not actually been with Jesus personally); and (2) They may have wondered if the Gentiles (who were rapidly becoming the majority in the Christian community) really were entitled to the same status in God's kingdom as they (the original Jewish believers) were. The parable's stress is on the fact that a person's status in the kingdom is a matter of God's grace and not a reward for the longevity of one's work for God.

20:1 to hire men to work in his vineyard. Landowners had full-time servants who took care of the daily needs of the estate, but at certain times (such as at planting, pruning or harvest) they would hire day laborers to help with work that the regular servants could not do on their own. At these times, men would gather in the village and hope that they might be hired.

vineyard. Since the Old Testament often used a vineyard as a metaphor for Israel (Isa. 5:1–7; Jer. 12:10), it may be that the vineyard here is meant to suggest Israel. The workers are then those who are called to care for (and tend to) Israel.

20:2 He agreed to pay them. The implication is that this was a negotiated arrangement. Bargaining back and forth was a common way for people in the Middle East to do business (as offers and counteroffers would be made). Since the landowner needed workers for that day, the laborers were in a position to negotiate a bit.

a denarius. This was a subsistence wage. Apparently this was considered a fair wage for a day's work.

20:3 the third hour. This would have been about 9 a.m.

doing nothing. By this time in the morning, if no one had hired the workers it was unlikely that they would get work that day.

the marketplace. This was the gathering place for a village. It would be a natural place for people looking for work to go in hopes of meeting someone who would be able to hire them.

20:4 I will pay you whatever is right. Since these workers had no reasonable prospects for work that day, they were not in much of a position to bargain. Whatever the landowner paid them would be better than nothing. There is no negotiation about the wage; just the promise that the landowner will not exploit them. Since those hired first agreed to a denarius, the expectation is set up among the listeners of the parable that these men would receive some fraction of that.

20:5 the sixth hour. This is noontime.

the ninth hour. This is 3 p.m. For the landowner to have to keep going to the marketplace to find workers indicates that the job (probably gathering a harvest) was more demanding than expected. It would be important to gather in a harvest as quickly as possible so it would not be spoiled by rain or rot.

20:6–7 This scene "recalls, implies, and summarizes the householder's previous dealings with 'the others'" (Scott).

20:6 the eleventh hour. This is 5 p.m. The listeners would have been surprised that the landowner was still hiring people this late in the day.

20:8–12 The landowner settles accounts with his workers. While the landowner's last-minute hiring would have been a surprise to the listeners, his method of payment would have been far more of a shock!

20:8 *When evening came.* This would be at dusk. The laborer's day went from sunrise to sunset.

beginning with the last ones hired and going on to the first. This arrangement sets up the scene that assures the confrontation of verses 11–12.

20:9–12 Probably those hired last agreed to the same arrangement with the landowner as those hired at the third hour (i.e., they would be paid "whatever is right"—v. 4). As they receive a denarius for an hour's work, they would have been joyfully surprised. Quite naturally, the spirits of the others in line would suddenly rise as they would assume their wages would be based on the same generous nature of the master—if those who worked only one hour or so received a denarius, what might those who had worked all day receive? Instead, as the foreman continues to pay each one a denarius, the earlier workers grow angry at the master. What at first seemed like a just and fair wage to which they could agree (v. 2) now appeared to them to be unjust and insulting.

20:12 *you have made them equal to us.* This is the crux of the complaint. The laborers assumed a hierarchal relationship to the master. Since they had been involved in working for him all day long, surely their reward ought to be greater than those who only got involved in the final hour. The parable shows that a concern for reward based on merit rather than on the grace of the master (God) is inappropriate in the kingdom.

20:13 *Friend.* In the other places where this form of address is used (Matt. 22:12; 26:50), it has an ironic twist to it. The laborers are not relating to the landowner as a friend, but as an unjust man.

I am not being unfair to you. The laborers' expressed concern was for justice. The landowner's point was that his actions were not unjust, since he was paying them what they had agreed to in the beginning. His generosity to the others cannot be interpreted as unfairness to them since he has fulfilled his promise to them.

20:15 *Don't I have the right to do what I want with my own money?* The landowner points out that he has the right to do what he will with his own money. The laborers are simply not in a position to tell him to whom he can or cannot be generous. In light of the ongoing conflict with the Pharisees regarding Jesus' interest in the religious outcasts of his time, Jesus, by means of this parable, "warns the Pharisees that a desire to live justly according to the covenant should not lead to an attitude that dictates to the covenant God how mercy and generosity should be shown. The line between following God's will and deciding what God wills is always thin and fragile" (Donahue).

Or are you envious because I am generous? Literally, "Is your eye evil because I am good?" The evil eye is warned against in Matthew 6:23. Both eye and heart are sometimes used in the Bible as a metaphor to describe the motivating principle that guides the way a person lives (see Ps. 119:36–37). The image of an "evil eye" was used to describe those who were greedy or stingy. Thus the "good eye" refers to people who have a generous spirit that leads them to share their material possessions. The contrast, therefore, is between those who live a life of generosity that rejoices in the good fortunes of others, and those who lead "a life in the dark, like a blind man, because the 'evil eye' of selfishness gives no light to show the way" (France). The jealousy of these men led them to consider this good man to be unjust.

20:16 This line, in reverse order of that in Matthew 19:30, connects the parable with the scene in 19:28–30. The promise that the disciples will judge over Israel (19:28) is not to be made into a new battleground for positions of status. The disciples are not to lord over one another (Matt. 20:25), but are to live as servants of God's people (Matt. 20:28).

12 Ten Virgins—Matthew 25:1–13

THREE-PART AGENDA

ICE-BREAKER
15 Minutes

BIBLE STUDY
30 Minutes

CARING TIME
15–45 Minutes

 LEADER: Has your group discussed its plans on what to study after this course is finished? What about the mission project described on page M6 in the center section?

TO BEGIN THE BIBLE STUDY TIME
(Choose 1 or 2)

1. What time do you usually go to bed at night?

2. What's your remedy for staying awake when you start getting drowsy?

3. When have you experienced a dead battery (or batteries) at an inopportune time?

READ SCRIPTURE & DISCUSS
(If you don't have time for all the questions in this section, conclude the Bible Study [30 min.] by answering question #7.)

1. What is one of your classic memories of being late and missing something important?

2. What makes some of the virgins "wise" and others "foolish"?

3. What would you call the refusal of the wise virgins to share their oil: Selfish? Shrewd? Unfair? Justified? Other?

4. From this parable, what two key points did Jesus want the listeners to know about his future return?

The Parable of the Ten Virgins

25 *"At that time the kingdom of heaven will be like ten virgins who took their lamps and went out to meet the bridegroom. ²Five of them were foolish and five were wise. ³The foolish ones took their lamps but did not take any oil with them. ⁴The wise, however, took oil in jars along with their lamps. ⁵The bridegroom was a long time in coming, and they all became drowsy and fell asleep.*

⁶"At midnight the cry rang out: 'Here's the bridegroom! Come out to meet him!'

⁷"Then all the virgins woke up and trimmed their lamps. ⁸The foolish ones said to the wise, 'Give us some of your oil; our lamps are going out.'

⁹" 'No,' they replied, 'there may not be enough for both us and you. Instead, go to those who sell oil and buy some for yourselves.'

¹⁰"But while they were on their way to buy the oil, the bridegroom arrived. The virgins who were ready went in with him to the wedding banquet. And the door was shut.

¹¹"Later the others also came. 'Sir! Sir!' they said. 'Open the door for us!'

¹²"But he replied, 'I tell you the truth, I don't know you.'

¹³"Therefore keep watch, because you do not know the day or the hour."

5. How does it make you feel to know the door to the kingdom gets closed for some?

6. How prepared do you feel for Christ's return?

7. What have you found helpful in keeping your lamp trimmed and full of oil?

CARING TIME

(Answer all the questions that follow, then close in prayer.)

1. Next week will be your last session in this study. How would you like to celebrate: A dinner? A party? Other?

2. What is the next step for this group: Start a new group? Continue with another study?

3. How can the group pray for you?

(If the group plans to continue, see the back inside cover of this book for what's available from Serendipity.)

Notes—Matthew 25:1–13

Summary. This is the first of three parables in Matthew 25 that deal with the return of the Lord on the Day of Judgment, a theme that dominates much of chapter 24 as well. The focus of this and the final two parables is on the need for the disciples to "keep watch" (v. 13), since the time for this day is unknown. The Parable of the Talents (25:14–30) stresses that watching means being occupied with investing one's God-given abilities in the work of the kingdom, while the final parable shows that such an investment means caring for the needy (25:31–46).

25:1 *ten virgins.* There is no attempt in the parable to impart any special meaning to the numbers 10 or five. They simply reflect two categories of people. It is not clear who these young women are: the attendants of the bride, servants in the groom's house, friends, or neighbors. In any case, their job is to escort the bridegroom in the wedding procession.

took their lamps. Since weddings typically occurred at night, lamps would both illuminate the bridal procession and add to the celebrative nature of the event. The lamps were probably small earthen jars with a wick inserted to draw the oil used as fuel. They would be held up on poles to brighten the way for the procession. Or they were torches made of rags wrapped around the end of a pole and soaked in oil. Such torches would burn for about 15 minutes and then would have to be dipped in oil again.

to meet the bridegroom. The parable is based upon common wedding practices of the time. Weddings typically took place in the house of the groom or in his parents' home. Prior to the actual ceremony, the groom would go to the home of the bride and lead her in a procession back to his house where the wedding would take place. In a village, the procession would be made up of everyone in the town! While commentators differ on the exact situation of these 10 women, a best guess is that they are either at the bride's house or are somewhere along the processional route waiting for the groom to come. In contrast to most other parables, the details of this parable are somewhat unrealistic (i.e., weddings did not occur at midnight; shops would not be open so late). This suggests that the parable is to be interpreted more as an allegory than is true for most of Jesus' parables. In an allegory, details do not just provide a story's context, but carry meaning in and of themselves. As a result,

sometimes unrealistic situations develop as a result of pressing the details to carry such a weight. As an allegory, the parable likely follows the lead of the Old Testament in picturing God (or, in this context, the Messiah) as the groom coming to take Israel as his bride (Isa. 54:4–5; 62:4; Ezek. 16:7; Hos. 2:19). The maidens are those who are to attend to God's people while they await the coming of the Lord.

25:2 *foolish … wise.* In Old Testament usage, wise people are those who live in accordance with God's law. They make good choices in life because they put truth into practice. Fools are those who hear truth but fail to act upon it (see also Matt. 7:24–27). The action of the foolish women in this parable is not an isolated event for them; rather it is indicative of the way they live their lives. They do not show forethought; they do not prepare for the future. In the context of the parable, they are like people who fail to be prepared for the coming of the Lord in judgment. Likewise, the wise women are habitually wise; in light of their future expectations, they make responsible decisions in the present.

25:3 *did not take any oil.* The only fuel for their lamps was whatever was left in the earthen lamps from the last use.

25:5 *The bridegroom was a long time in coming.* The early church expected Jesus to return in glory fairly soon after his ascension. Many of the parables related to the return of the Lord can be seen as being intended to warn against that expectation (Matt. 24:43,48; 25:14ff). The time frame is ambiguous.

they all became drowsy and fell asleep. There is no suggestion that their falling asleep was inappropriate; it simply accents how long they had to wait.

25:6 *At midnight.* Just as it would be today, this was late for a wedding! It emphasizes how delayed the groom was in arriving, since this would have been long after most people would have expected him.

the cry rang out. In a village, everyone would be waiting for the celebration to begin. At first sight of the groom, the word would spread through the town.

Come out to meet him! People would gather around the groom to escort him to the bride's home

and then back to the actual site of the wedding. His unexpected arrival, the shout of proclamation, and the people coming out to meet him all suggest pictures used to describe the final return of Christ (see 1 Thess. 4:16–17).

25:7 *trimmed their lamps.* This is, literally, "put their torches in order." This would include dipping them in oil again or making sure there was oil in the lamps and then setting them alight for the procession. The lamps of the foolish virgins would not stay lit for lack of adequate oil.

25:8 *our lamps are going out.* Now that the time for the procession has arrived, the foolish women realize they do not have adequate supplies to keep their lamps burning. Following the allegorical interpretation of this parable, the lamps may be meant to indicate the good deeds of believers that spring from faith (see Matt. 5:16). The foolish women are those who have no good deeds with which to greet the Lord.

25:9 *No.* The wise women's refusal to share was not selfish, but simply prudent. They carried only enough for themselves. To share meant everyone would not have sufficient fuel. This aspect of the story is thought to show that each person needs his or her own relationship with the Lord; such a relationship cannot be obtained by simply being around those who demonstrate faith through faithful living.

go to those who sell oil. Since it is so late, it would be very difficult to find a shopkeeper willing to open shop and sell oil. At the time of the Lord's return, it is too late to try to make up for one's lack of preparation beforehand.

25:10 *the wedding banquet.* The image of a wedding feast was commonly used to describe God's salvation of his people (Mark 2:19; Luke 14:15).

the door was shut. Here the parable clearly moves from a story about a typical wedding to the messianic banquet, as latecomers would not be excluded from a regular wedding party. The shutting of the door to the banquet would strike the hearers as

unusual, forcing them to consider the meaning of the parable. This aspect of the parable emphasizes the urgency of one's response to the Lord. There is a limited time when the "day of salvation" is extended to people: It must be received while the Lord provides the opportunity (see also Matt. 7:22–23; Luke 13:35).

25:12 When the foolish women finally arrived, they were forbidden entry.

I don't know you. See also Matthew 7:23 and Luke 13:25,27; the latter is found in a short parable that has similarities to the story of the 10 virgins. This is the final word of rejection of the Lord to those who fail to be ready for his coming. While they have the outward signs of commitment, their unpreparedness demonstrates their lack of taking his teachings seriously. In this context, not to be known does not mean that these women are not recognized, but that they are not really part of the company of people who are friends with the groom.

25:13 *Therefore keep watch.* This is an editorial comment added to apply the parable to the situation of the listeners. The fact that all the maidens fell asleep does not violate the meaning of this call. The wise women were prepared nonetheless. They had kept watch by making adequate and appropriate preparations. The foolish had neglected their responsibilities. When the time for action came, they were not ready. While the allegorical nature of this parable means that many lessons may be implied in it (such as the fact that faith cannot be transferred from one person to another, there is a limited opportunity in which to enter the kingdom of God, and the last day will arrive unexpectedly), the main application Matthew draws from it is to encourage the disciples to be vigilant and prepared for the coming of the Lord. The following parables show what such preparation for the kingdom of God involves.

you do not know the day or the hour. This is a steady theme in the New Testament teachings about the return of the Lord (Matt. 24:36,44; Mark 13:35; Luke 12:40; 1 Thess. 5:1–2).

13 Weeds—Matthew 13:24–30,36–43

THREE-PART AGENDA

ICE-BREAKER
15 Minutes

BIBLE STUDY
30 Minutes

CARING TIME
15–45 Minutes

 LEADER: Check page M7 of the center section for a good ice-breaker for this last session.

TO BEGIN THE BIBLE STUDY TIME
(Choose 1 or 2)

1. What weeds have you had to battle the most in your garden or yard?

2. If you were a farmer, what crop would you like to grow?

3. As a teenager, what tricks did you play on someone while they were sleeping?

READ SCRIPTURE & DISCUSS
(If you don't have time for all the questions in this section, conclude the Bible Study [30 min.] by answering question #7.)

1. How has this group, or someone in the group, been a blessing to you over the course of this study?

2. In Jesus' interpretation of this parable for his disciples, what does he say the various elements in the story represent?

3. What was the enemy trying to accomplish by sowing bad seed in with the good?

4. Why did the owner of the field not have his servants go and pull out the weeds immediately?

The Parable of the Weeds

²⁴Jesus told them another parable: "The kingdom of heaven is like a man who sowed good seed in his field. ²⁵But while everyone was sleeping, his enemy came and sowed weeds among the wheat, and went away. ²⁶When the wheat sprouted and formed heads, then the weeds also appeared.

²⁷"The owner's servants came to him and said, 'Sir, didn't you sow good seed in your field? Where then did the weeds come from?'

²⁸" 'An enemy did this,' he replied.

"The servants asked him, 'Do you want us to go and pull them up?'

²⁹" 'No,' he answered, 'because while you are pulling the weeds, you may root up the wheat with them. ³⁰Let both grow together until the harvest. At that time I will tell the harvesters: First collect the weeds and tie them in bundles to be burned; then gather the wheat and bring it into my barn.' " ...

The Parable of the Weeds Explained

³⁶Then he left the crowd and went into the house. His disciples came to him and said, "Explain to us the parable of the weeds in the field."

³⁷He answered, "The one who sowed the good seed is the Son of Man. ³⁸The field is the world, and the good seed stands for the sons of the kingdom. The weeds are the sons of the evil one, ³⁹and the enemy who sows them is the devil. The harvest is the end of the age, and the harvesters are angels.

⁴⁰"As the weeds are pulled up and burned in the fire, so it will be at the end of the age. ⁴¹The Son of Man will send out his angels, and they will weed out of his kingdom everything that causes sin and all who do evil. ⁴²They will throw them into the fiery furnace, where there will be weeping and gnashing of teeth. ⁴³Then the righteous will shine like the sun in the kingdom of their Father. He who has ears, let him hear."

5. What happens to the weeds and wheat "at the end of the age" (v. 40)?

6. In this study of Jesus' parables, what has been the key lesson you have learned?

7. On a scale of 1 (baby steps) to 10 (giant leaps), how has your relationship with God progressed over the last three months?

CARING TIME

(Answer all the questions that follow, then close in prayer.)

1. What will you remember most about this group?

2. What has the group decided to do next? What is the next step for you personally?

3. How would you like the group to continue to pray for you?

Notes—Matthew 13:24–30,36–43

Summary. The Parable of the Weeds is the first of three parables about the growth of the kingdom. It is followed by the Parable of the Mustard Seed (Matt. 13:31–32) and the Parable of the Yeast (Matt. 13:33). All communicate that the kingdom of God will assuredly grow, although by a process that is hard to discern (and may at first look ineffectual).

13:24–30 The issue to which this parable speaks is the fact that (contrary to popular opinion), the kingdom of God will not be ushered in suddenly, with a great cataclysmic explosion. Popular expectation held that God's kingdom would be established by means of a dramatic act of judgment that would divide humanity into two camps: the sons of light and the sons of darkness. With the coming of Jesus, however, life appeared to go on much as it always had. There was no apocalyptic revelation of God, no war that wiped out the wicked, no sudden deliverance for the righteous. Some people believed and practiced what he taught and others did not ... and nothing happened to those who did not! Even more confusing, within his ranks there were some whose allegiance was questionable. How could he claim to be the herald of God's kingdom? Yet in Jesus the kingdom is begun. However, its full nature and extent will not be made known until the Day of Judgment. For the time being, the kingdom of God is hidden (France) and his disciples must not be occupied with thoughts of how to purify it by their own efforts. God will take that action at the time of the final judgment. An explanation for the parable is given in verses 36–43.

13:24 *Jesus told them another parable.* In Matthew, this parable follows the Parable of the Sower. Both parables use an agricultural image to teach about the certain growth and productivity of the kingdom of God.

The kingdom of heaven. In their desire not to take the name of the Lord their God in vain (Ex. 20:7), Jews avoided direct references to God at all. Instead, they would refer to God through a phrase like "the One in heaven." The "kingdom of heaven" is simply a substitution for the "kingdom of God."

13:25 *sleeping.* This does not suggest inattention, but simply normal rest. It is the same as saying that the deed was done "at night."

weeds. This was probably darnel, a poisonous weed that looks like wheat until the time when the head forms on the wheat. Sowing a field with useless seed was a common means by which a disgruntled person might seek revenge upon an enemy, since such a sowing could devastate a crop. To sow darnel among wheat was forbidden by Roman law.

13:27 *didn't you sow good seed.* "The question, although quite natural from the agricultural point of view, may also indicate the application of the parable to the situation of the church of Matthew's day. It was probably experiencing concern at the apparent lack of triumph and progress in the world of the kingdom inaugurated by Jesus" (Hill).

13:29 It might have been possible to pull out the darnel when it was young. However, its close resemblance to wheat meant that some of the young wheat would inadvertently get uprooted as well. When the plant was more mature—especially if there were a lot of it—its root system would be so intertwined with that of the wheat that to uproot it would also uproot a good bit of the wheat. Thus, the owner of the field chooses to do nothing. He neither tries to pull out the weeds, nor seeks to find out who did this so that he might get revenge. To the surprise of his servants (and the hearers of the story), he simply allows the wheat and the weeds to grow up together.

> *The Son of Man, who sowed the good seed (v. 37), is also the one who harvests the crop and owns the kingdom.*

13:30 Only at the time of the harvest, when the fruit of each plant was clearly visible, would the weeds be separated from the wheat. The darnel (sometimes used for fuel when there was a shortage of wood) would be burned up while the wheat would go into the barn for storage and later use.

13:36–43 One of Matthew's themes is the coming judgment of God, in which the righteous will be vin-

dicated and the wicked punished (3:7–12; 7:24–27; 10:23; 11:20–24; 18:7–9; 22:1–14; 24:1–51; 25:31–46). This was an important expectation for the Jewish communities of the time and was embraced by many of the early Christians as well. Such a destiny calls for repentance and a life of obedience to God.

13:37–39 What the various elements of the parable mean are explained.

13:37 the Son of Man. This is an allusion to the heavenly figure in Daniel 7:13–14, who is given authority by God over all the world.

13:38 the world. This is secular reality; it refers to the present age.

sons of the kingdom. These are the people who have been given the gift of the kingdom (Matt. 5:3). To be a "son" of something or someone meant to be a person who reflects the characteristics of that particular thing or person. The "sons of the kingdom" are people whose lives are in conformity to the values of that kingdom. The "sons of the evil one" are those whose character reflects that of Satan.

13:39 The harvest. Picturing God's final judgment in terms of a harvest was a common metaphor in the Old Testament and other apocalyptic literature (Isa. 17:4–6; Jer. 51:33; Joel 3:12–13).

the end of the age. Apocalyptic literature viewed history in terms of "the present age" and "the age to come." The present age is marked by sin and the oppression of the righteous, but the "age to come" will begin when God dramatically puts an end to this age by his judgment and eradication of evil, ushering in a new age in which he reigns over all with justice and peace.

angels. Angels figure prominently in apocalyptic scenes of God's judgment as the agents through which that judgment is executed (v. 41; Dan. 7:10; 2 Thess. 1:7; Rev. 15:1; 16:1; 18:1,21).

13:40 burned in the fire. God's judgment was often described in terms of a consuming fire that would purify the world of all evil (2 Thess. 1:7; 2 Peter 3:10; Rev. 19:20).

13:41 The Son of Man, who sowed the good seed (v. 37), is also the one who harvests the crop and owns the kingdom.

13:42 weeping and gnashing of teeth. This is a stock phrase used to indicate the extreme horror and suffering of those who experience God's wrath. In Matthew, such a punishment is described in terms of a fire (here and v. 50), darkness (8:12; 22:13; 25:30), and being cut to pieces (24:51).

13:43 the righteous. These are the "sons of the kingdom" (v. 38) who heard the word and practiced it. Although their identity was once hidden (when the wheat and the weeds were growing together), they will be fully revealed in the age to come as those who share God's character.

shine like the sun. Light is often used to describe the nature of holiness. It is a positive characteristic, as opposed to the darkness that marks the nature of sin (Dan. 12:3; 1 John 1:5).

He who has ears, let him hear. This is another stock phrase used to call people to think about what they have heard: What does it mean? What are its implications? How are we to act upon this story? The worst condition to be in is one in which we hear Jesus' words but fail to let them have an effect on our lives.

> *Light is often used to describe the nature of holiness. It is a positive characteristic, as opposed to the darkness that marks the nature of sin.*

Notes (cont.)

"Let both grow together until the harvest."

"… The visible church is to have its intermixture of good and bad until the end of time, and by consequence … the fact of the bad being found mingled with the good will in no wise justify a separation from it, or an attempt to set up a little Church of our own. Where men attempt this … it is not difficult to see what fatal effects on their own spiritual life it must have, what darkness it must bring upon them, and into what a snare of pride it must cast them. For while even in the best men there is the same intermixture of good and evil as there is outwardly in the Church, such conduct will infallibly lead a man to the willful shutting his eyes both to the evil which is in himself, and in the little schismatical body he will then call the Church, since only so the attempt will even seem to be successful.

"Not that there is not something in every man which inclines him to (this) error … Nay, it would argue little love or holy earnestness in him, if he had not this longing to see the Church of his Savior a glorious Church without spot or wrinkle. But he must learn that the desire, righteous and holy as in itself it is, yet is not to find its fulfillment in this present evil time … He learns that all self-willed and impatient attempts, such as have been repeated again and again, to anticipate that perfect communion of saints are indeed works of the flesh, and that however well they may promise at the first, no blessing will rest upon them, nor will they for long even appear to be attended with success" (*Notes on the Parables of Our Lord*, by Richard Trench, New York: D. Appleton and Co., 1864, pp. 85–86).

Acknowledgments

It is not possible (nor desirable) to tackle as formidable a subject as the Parables of Jesus without the aid of others. The standard exegetical tools have, of course, been used: The Arndt and Gingrich *Greek-English Lexicon of the New Testament; The Interpreter's Dictionary of the Bible,* etc. In addition, reference has been made to a series of fine commentaries: Albright, W.F. and Mann, C.S., *Matthew*, (The Anchor Bible), Garden City, NY: Doubleday, 1971. Bailey, Kenneth E., *Poet and Peasant: Through Peasant Eyes*, Grand Rapids, MI: Eerdmans, 1983. Barclay, William, *The Gospel of Luke* (The Daily Study Bible Series), Philadelphia, PA: The Westminster Press, 1976 (Second Edition). Donahue, John R., *The Gospel in Parable*, Philadelphia, PA, Fortress Press, 1988. Drury, John, *The Parables in the Gospels*, New York, NY: Crossroad, 1989. Ellis, E. Earle, *The Gospel of Luke* (The New Century Bible Commentary), Grand Rapids, MI: Eerdmans, 1981. Geldenhuys, J. Norval, *Commentary on the Gospel of Luke* (The New London Commentary on the New Testament), London: Marshal, Morgan, and Scott, 1950. Hendriksen, William, *The Gospel of Luke* (New Testament Commentary) Grand Rapids, MI: Baker Book House, 1978. Hill, David, *The Gospel of Matthew*, (The New Century Bible Commentary), Grand Rapids, MI: Eerdmans, 1981. Marshall, I. Howard, *Commentary on Luke* (The New International Greek Testament Commentary), Grand Rapids, MI: Eerdmans Publishing Co., 1978. Mounce, Robert H., *Matthew*, (A Good News Commentary), San Francisco, CA: Harper and Row, 1985. Perkins, Pheme, *Hearing the Parables of Jesus*, New York, NY: Paulist Press, 1981. Scott, Bernard Brandon, *Hear Then The Parable*, Minneapolis, MN: Fortress Press, 1989. Trench, Richard, *Notes on the Parables of Our Lord*, New York, NY: D. Appleton and Co., 1864.

Caring Time Notes